Conversational RUSSIAN in 7 Days

Master Language Survival Skills in Just One Week!

Shirley Baldwin and Sarah Boas

McGraw-Hill

New York Chicago San Francisco Lisbon London Madrid Mexico City Milan New Delhi San Juan Seoul Singapore Sydney Toronto

The McGraw-Hill Companies

Originally published by Hodder & Stoughton Publishers.

4 5 6 7 8 9 0 WKT/WKT 2 1 0 9 8 7 6

ISBN 0-07-143281-7 (package)
0-07-143280-9 (book)

Acknowledgments
The authors and publishers are grateful to the following for supplying photographs: S. Baldwin, Barnaby's Picture Library, J. Allan Cash Ltd., J. Lowe, E. Mungall, Spectrum Colour Library.

McGraw-Hill books are available at special quantity discounts to use as premiums and sales promotions, or for use in corporate training programs. For more information, please write to the Director of Special Sales, Professional Publishing, McGraw-Hill, Two Penn Plaza, New York, NY 10121-2298. Or contact your local bookstore.

This book is printed on acid-free paper.

CONTENTS

INTRODUCTION

Conversational Russian in 7 Days is a short course in Russian that will equip you to deal with everyday situations when you visit the Soviet Union: shopping, asking for directions, changing money, using the phone, and so on.

The course is divided into 7 units, each corresponding to a day in the lives of the members of a school party and a cultural tour during their week in the Soviet Union. Each unit is based on a dialogue, which introduces the essential language items in context. Key phrases are highlighted in the dialogues, and the phrasebook section that follows lists these and other useful phrases and tells you what they are in English.

Within the units there are also short informational sections in English on the topics covered, sections giving basic grammatical explanations, and a number of follow-up activities designed to be useful as well as fun. Answers can be checked in a key at the back of the book. Two cassettes are also available to help you practice your Russian.

BEFORE YOU LEAVE

One of the major problems facing visitors to the USSR is coming to grips with the Cyrillic alphabet. In fact, this is not nearly as difficult as it seems, and it is certainly worth spending some time making yourself familiar with it before setting out on your trip. If you do, you will be surprised at just how many road signs, street names, metro stations, and so on you will be able to read.

The Russian alphabet

Letter	*Sound*	*Example*			
А а	*a*	as in *father*	**Р р**	*r*	as in *rat*
Б б	*b*	as in *bat*	**С с**	*s*	as in *sand*
В в	*v*	as in *vet*	**Т т**	*t*	as in *tree*
Г г	*g*	as in *girl*	**У у**	*oo*	as in *shoot*
Д д	*d*	as in *dog*	**Ф ф**	*f*	as in *foot*
Е е	*ye*	as in *yet*	**Х х**	sim. to *ch* in *loch*	
Ё ё	*yo*	as in *yonder*	**Ц ц**	*ts*	as in *pets*
Ж ж	*su*	as in *pleasure*	**Ч ч**	*ch*	as in *chap*
З з	*z*	as in *zoo*	**Ш ш**	*sh*	as in *shop*
И и	*ee*	as in *keep*	**Щ щ**	*shch*	as in *fresh cheese*
Й й	*y*	as in *toy*	**Ъ ъ***	hard sign (not pron.)	
К к	*k*	as in *king*	**Ы ы**	sim. to *i* in *fit*	
Л л	*l*	as in *bottle*	**Ь ь***	soft sign, see note	
М м	*m*	as in *mat*	**Э э**	*e*	as in *bell*
Н н	*n*	as in *net*	**Ю ю**	*you*	as in *youth*
О о	*o*	as in *for*	**Я я**	*ya*	as in *yarn*
П п	*p*	as in *pot*			

ай is pronounced *eye*, **ей** is *yei*, and **ой** is pronounced *oi*.

* The hard sign (**ъ**) is not pronounced, but it is sometimes found between a consonant and a vowel to indicate that these should be pronounced separately. The soft sign (**ь**) at the end of a word softens the preceding consonant and produces a sound similar to a short *y* (as in *yet*).

Pronunciation

1 Russian is a strongly stressed language, with stress always falling upon one syllable of a word (unfortunately, only experience will tell you which!). Vowels that are not stressed are pronounced slightly differently from vowels that carry the stress—they are spoken more quickly and tend to lose their value. Most notable is unstressed **о**, pronounced almost like an unstressed **a**: водá *vada* (water); unstressed **е** and **я** are pronounced almost like an **i**: теáтр *tiatr*. In the text, you will find stress marks (´) that indicate the stressed syllable in each word.
2 You will see from the transliteration that some consonants at the end of words are pronounced slightly differently from the way in which they are written, e.g., хле**б** *khlyep* (bread), and some consonants may have special pronunciations in a few words, e.g., се**г**óдня *sivodnya* (today).
3 R (**Р**) is rolled in Russian.
4 The transliteration used in this book follows the English sounds as far as possible. Note however that **kh** is the sound *ch* in *loch*, and **zh** is the sound *su* in *pleasure*.

things to do

1 Some Russian letters are very similar to English. Look quickly at the alphabet and notice which letters look the same as or similar to English ones. Now see if you can read these words, and have a guess at their meaning:

комéта	дáма	балéт	такт	табáк	котлéта
кафé	факт	мáма	фóто	дáта	áтом
болт	кóфе	баллáда	кóма	блок	кадéт

2 Here are some more words in which all the letters are similar to English ones. See if you can read them (check in the key that you have pronounced them correctly):

да (yes)	дом (house)	дéло (business)
кто (who)	как (how)	там (there)
э́то (this)	молокó (milk)	так (so)
тéло (body)	мóда (fashion)	мáло (little, few)

3 These words all sound very similar to their English equivalents. Look at the alphabet and figure out how to pronounce them (if you are right, you will also be able to say what they mean!):

такси́	парк	кли́ник	фильм	вóдка
телефóн	ви́за	буфéт	банк	туалéт
вестибю́ль	тури́ст	динáмо	метрó	студéнт
трáктор	центр	концéрт	винó	газéта

AT CUSTOMS

Arriving at the airport When arriving in the Soviet Union, you will need to pass through passport control and customs. Both of these can involve lines and delays, as officials are meticulous in scrutinizing passport details and will often examine luggage very thoroughly. Have your passport, your visa, and your customs declaration handy—and make sure they have been returned to you before you move on.

таможня/customs

Customs officials will not necessarily speak English, so listen for these words:

деклара́ция *diklaratsiya* declaration
па́спорт *paspart* passport
ви́за *viza* visa
бага́ж *bagazh* luggage
валю́та *valyoota* currency
заяви́ть *zayavit* to declare
откро́йте чемода́н *atkroitye chemadan* open your case

But probably the most important words you need to know are:

да *da* yes **нет** *nyet* no

Customs regulations There are quite a number of items you're not allowed to bring into or take out of the country (for details, consult Intourist). Among the things you can't take in are hallucinatory drugs and narcotics, Soviet currency, goods carried for someone else, any kind of pornography, and books, films, etc., that could be detrimental in any way to the interests of the Soviet Union. You can bring in and take out small quantities of wine, spirits, and cigarettes, and the normal personal effects, travel goods, and food for the journey. If you're thinking of taking more than two cameras and such things as video recording equipment, it's best to check first.

All foreign currency and checks, jewelry, and other valuables have to be registered on a customs declaration when you enter the country, and the form stamped. Be sure to keep your customs declaration safe throughout your stay as you won't be able to take your currency and valuables out again without it, and if you lose the declaration *it won't be replaced*. (If you're coming ashore from a cruise, you don't need to fill out a customs declaration.)

When leaving, you can bring out inexpensive souvenirs, jewelry, furs, etc., bought in hard currency shops (keep the receipts), but among the things you can't bring out are Soviet currency, state loan certificates, etc., works of art and antiques (such as icons, pictures, furniture, carpets, coins, books) of artistic, historic, cultural, or scientific interest. These can only be exported with the permission of the Soviet Ministry of Culture and on payment of customs duty (equal to the full purchase price of the goods). Undeclared currency or other items are liable to confiscation, along with any vehicle in which they were hidden.

Note that you cannot bring **Soviet currency** into the country nor take it out, so if you change more rubles than you need you will have to change them back again and are likely to lose out on the deal. Most hotels used by foreigners as well as shops, bars, and restaurants take hard currency, so it is advisable to change only a small amount of money into rubles and be prepared to spend it all. Note also that it is illegal to sell foreign currency to individuals.

ПОНЕДЕЛЬНИК MONDA

SAYING HELLO AND GOOD-BYE

After passing through customs, you will be met by the Intourist guide assigned to your group. If you are on your own, look for the Intourist desk where you will be given instructions about what transportation has been arranged to take you to your hotel.

приезд/the arrival

Mike Nash, a teacher of Russian, and his daughter Alice (16) arrive at Leningrad's airport with a party of students at the beginning of a week's tour of the Soviet Union. They are greeted by their Soviet guide, Lena.

Lena:	**Извини́те пожа́луйста, вы** ми́стер Наш? *Izvinitye, pazhalasta, vy mister Nash?*	Excuse me, please, are you Mr. Nash?
Mike:	**Да, я.** *Da, ya.*	Yes, I am.
Lena:	**Здра́вствуйте!** Я Ле́на, ваш гид. *Zdrastvuitye! Ya Lyena, vash geed.*	Hello. I'm Lena, your guide.
Mike:	**О́чень прия́тно.** Вот А́лис, моя́ до́чь. *Ochen priyatna. Vot Alice, maya doch.*	Pleased to meet you. Here's Alice, my daughter.
Lena:	Ах, э́то ва́ша дочь? **До́брое у́тро.** *Ach, eta vasha doch? Dobraye ootra.*	Ah, that's your daughter? Good morning.
Alice:	До́брое у́тро. *Dobraye ootra.*	Good morning.

Как вас зову́т? *What's your name?*

You will find that most people in the Soviet Union have three names, the middle one (patronymic) taken from the father's first name, e.g., Konstantín Pávlovich Ivanóv. Among Russians, the polite form of address is to use the first two names only. However, generally speaking you can call people you meet such as guides, waiters, etc., by their first names. For business purposes, it is acceptable to use the terms **ми́стер/ми́ссис/мисс** (Mr./Mrs./Miss) followed by the person's last name. You may also occasionally hear the words **господи́н/госпожа́** (*gaspadin/gaspazha*) plus a surname for Mr./Mrs., as well as **това́рищ** *tavarishch* (comrade) or **колле́га** *kalyega* (colleague).

Как вас зову́т?	*Kak vas zavoot?*	What's your name?
Извини́те, вы . . .?	*Izvinitye, vy . . .?*	Excuse me, are you . . .?
Да, я.	*Da, ya.*	Yes, it's me.
Я . . .	*Ya . . .*	I'm . . .
Меня́ зову́т . . .	*Minya zavoot . . .*	My name is . . .
Я не . . .	*Ya ni . . .*	I'm not . . .

Как ва́ше и́мя/ ва́ша фами́лия?	*Kak vashe imya/ vasha familiya?*	What's your first name/ last name?
О́чень прия́тно.	*Ochen priyatna.*	Pleased to meet you. (lit. "Very pleasant")

Greetings and farewells

You should always shake hands when introduced to someone in the Soviet Union, and you might like to say:

Здра́вствуйте!	*Zdrastvuitye!*	Hello!
Как вы пожива́ете?	*Kak vy pazheevaetye?*	How are you?
Как дела́?	*Kak dyela?*	How are things?

To say, "Fine, thank you," use the Russian word for "good": **хорошо́** *kharasho.* **Здра́вствуйте** is only used for the first time in the day you meet somone. After that you can say:

До́брое у́тро.	*Dobraye utra.*	Good morning.
До́брый день.	*Dobriy den.*	Good afternoon.
До́брый ве́чер.	*Dobriy vyecher.*	Good evening.

The Russian for "good-bye" is **до свида́ния** *da svidaniya.*

Please and thank you

You will hear the Russian word for please, **пожа́луйста** *pazhalasta,* a great deal as it also means "pardon" and "don't mention it" (like the German "bitte"). For "thank you," say:

Спаси́бо.	*Spaseeba.*	Thank you.*
Спаси́бо большо́е.	*Spaseeba balshoye.*	Thank you very much.

*Take care; it can also mean "no, thank you" when declining a request (simply add **да** *da* or **нет** *nyet* to make your meaning clear).

REGISTERING AT A HOTEL

Hotels The cheapest way to visit the Soviet Union is to join an organized trip, either through Intourist or through one of the Soviet trade or educational organizations. However, it is possible to travel independently, and Intourist keeps a list of hotel rates in the major cities. Prices,which generally include breakfast and porterage, are not cheap for foreigners, and transfer from the airport or station is extra. You should book well ahead (hotels are particularly full from July to September when you may not find a single room) as only when your reservation is confirmed will you be issued a visa. Accommodation is free for children under 2, and in some categories of room, children up to 12 pay only for meals.

You will have booked and paid for your hotel before leaving for the Soviet Union, and probably you won't know exactly which hotel you'll be staying at until you actually arrive at the airport. Accommodations can be in one of the following categories: Suite, Deluxe, First Class, or Tourist Class. Many tours book visitors into First Class rooms with a bath or shower, toilets and telephone. However, apartments with up to 4 rooms are available at some hotels, and the more expensive accommodations include TV, radio, refrigerator, and use of car and driver.

On arriving you should hand in your accommodation voucher (or your guide will attend to this) and you may be asked to fill in a registration form (**регистрацио́нный лист** *registratsyonniy leest*) and hand over your passport, which will be returned to you later. After registering you will be given a hotel pass (**про́пуск** *propusk*) or a card (**ка́рточка** *kartachka*) that should be handed to the

дежу́рная *dyezhoornaya*—the attendant (usually female) who keeps the keys on each floor of the hotel. In smaller hotels you collect your key directly from the desk, but in large hotels catering exclusively to foreign tourists, you will not be allowed past the entrance desk without first showing your pass.

Tipping is officially discouraged and your hotel bill will include a service charge, but hotel staff, waiters, taxi-drivers, etc., have come to regard a small tip of say 5% to 10% as normal.

в гостинице/at the hotel

The party transfers by coach to the hotel, where Mike speaks to the desk clerk.

Mike: Здра́вствуйте. **Меня́ зову́т Наш—вот мой па́спорт**.
Zdrastvuitye. Minya zavoot Nash—vot moi paspart.

Clerk: Ми́стер Наш? . . . Но́мер два́дцать, на второ́м этаже́.
Mister Nash? . . . Nomir dvatsat, na ftarom etazhé.

Mike: **На како́м этаже́?**
Na kakom etazhé?

Clerk: На второ́м—вот ваш ключ.
Э́то ваш чемода́н? Лифт вон там . . .
Na ftarom—vot vash klyooch.
Eta vash chemadan? Lift von tam . . .

Mike: **Спаси́бо**.
Spaseeba.

Clerk: Пожа́луйста.
Pazhalasta.

Вот мой па́спорт/ваш ключ.	Here's my passport/your key.
на второ́м этаже́	on the second floor
Лифт вон там.	The elevator is there.

Asking about your room

Како́й но́мер?	*Kakoi nomir?*	Which room (number)?
но́мер два́дцать	*nomir dvatsat*	room number 20
одина́рный но́мер	*adinarniy nomir*	a single room
двойно́й но́мер	*dvoinoi nomir*	a double room

но́мер с ва́нной/ду́шем/телефо́ном *nomir s vannoy/dushem/tilifonam*	a room with a bath/shower/ telephone
но́мер с телеви́зором/холоди́льником *nomir s tiliveezaram/khaladilnikam*	a room with a TV/refrigerator

As well as keeping the keys, the **дежу́рная** will bring you cups of tea and run errands for you. If there is anything you need, you can try asking her to obtain it for you.

Принеси́те мне пожа́луйста полоте́нце. *Prinesitye mnye pazhalasta palatentse.*	Bring me a towel, please.
. . . одея́ло, поду́шку, мы́ло *. . . adeyala, padooshkoo, myla*	. . . a blanket, a pillow, soap

and when trying to find your way around, you can ask:
Где *Gdye* Where . . .?

Где туале́т/ва́нная/лифт? *Gdye twalyet/vannaya/lift?*	Where's the toilet/bathroom/elevator?
Где столо́вая/бар/буфе́т? *Gdye stalovaya/bar/boofyet?*	Where's the dining room/bar/buffet?

Note that the voltage in most Soviet hotels is 220 V.

На како́м этаже́? *On what floor?*

It is important to be able to use numbers in Russian—then you will feel confident when changing money, shopping, asking for your hotel key, and so on:

1	**оди́н/одна́/одно́*** *adin/adna/adno*	11	**оди́ннадцать** *adinatsat*
2	**два/две*** *dva/dvye*	12	**двена́дцать** *dvinatsat*
3	**три** tree	13	**трина́дцать** *treenatsat*
4	**четы́ре** *chitirye*	14	**четы́рнадцать** *chitirnatsat*
5	**пять** *pyat*	15	**пятна́дцать** *pitnatsat*
6	**шесть** *shest*	16	**шестна́дцать** *shisnatsat*
7	**семь** *syem*	17	**семна́дцать** *simnatsat*
8	**во́семь** *vosyem*	18	**восемна́дцать** *vosimnatsat*
9	**де́вять** *dyevyat*	19	**девятна́дцать** *divyatnatsat*
10	**де́сять** *dyesyat*	20	**два́дцать** *dvatsat*

*Note that the number "one" varies according to whether the noun is masculine, feminine, or neuter—see "the way it works" below. The number "two" is **два** for masculine and neuter nouns, **две** for feminine nouns.

If you want to talk about which floor your room is on, you will need to know how to say first, second, third, etc.:

на пе́рвом этаже́ *na pyervam etazhé*	on the 1st floor	**на тре́тьем этаже́** *na tryetim etazhé*	on the 3rd floor
на второ́м этаже́ *na ftarom etazhé*	on the 2nd floor	**на четвёртом этаже́** *na chitviortam etazhé*	on the 4th floor
		на пятом этаже *na pyatom etazhe*	on the 5th floor

(Note that the first floor in Russian is the equivalent of the first or ground floor in the United States, rather than the first floor above the ground, as in many European countries.) For a complete list of numbers, see p. 113.

Hotel services If you are traveling with a group, the price of the tour will include transfer from the airport to the hotel and porterage. Many of the large Intourist hotels offer the facilities seen in the illustration. You will be able to buy souvenirs, cards and stamps, newspapers, and pharmaceuticals. At the service bureau, you can obtain information, arrange to go on excursions, book tickets for the theater, concerts, ballet, etc., and order a car. The bureau is generally open from 9 a.m. to 9 p.m.

парикма́херская	beauty salon
са́уна	sauna
апте́ка	pharmacy
буфе́т	snack bar
банк	bank
бар	bar
рестора́н	restaurant
бюро́ обслу́живания	service bureau
по́чта	post
кио́ск	newsstand

the way it works

People and things (nouns)

The words for people and things in Russian are either masculine, feminine, or neuter. Generally speaking, words ending in a consonant or **й** are masculine, those ending in **а**, **я**, or **ия** are feminine, and those ending in **о**, **е**, or **ие** are neuter:

па́спорт (m.) *paspart* passport	**валю́та** (f.) *valyoota* (foreign) currency	**у́тро** (n.) *ootra* morning

My and your (possessive adjectives)

"My" and "your" are adjectives, and in Russian adjectives have to agree with the noun they accompany:

masculine	*feminine*	*neuter*
мой бага́ж *moi bagazh* my luggage	**моя́** су́мка *maya soomka* my bag	**моё** окно́ *mayo akno* my window
ваш чемода́н *vash chemadan* your case	**ва́ша** гости́ница *vasha gastinitsa* your hotel	**ва́ше** одея́ло *vashe adeyala* your blanket

I am, you are (the verb "to be")

The verb "to be" is generally omitted in Russian, so you would say:

Я ваш гид.	*Ya vash geed.*	I am your guide.
Вы ми́стер Наш.	*Vy mister Nash.*	You are Mr. Nash.

To ask a question, simply use a questioning tone of voice:

Вы ми́стер Смит?	*Vy mister Smeet?*	Are you Mr. Smith?

and to say no, you're not, use **не** *ni*:

Нет, я не ми́стер Смит.	*Nyet, ya ni mister Smeet.*	No, I'm not Mr. Smith.

Вот

Вот means "here is" or "there is." Use it like this:

Вот моя́ дочь.*	*Vot maya doch.*	Here's/there's my daughter.
Вот мой па́спорт.	*Vot moy paspart.*	Here's my passport.
Вот ваш ключ.	*Vot vash klyooch.*	Here's your key.

*A large number of words ending in a soft sign (**ь**) are feminine.

things to do

1.1 **Pronunciation practice** These are some of the signs you may come across in the Soviet Union, perhaps at your hotel. See if you can pronounce them (look at the Key to see if you were right!).

1 РЕСТОРА́Н	**2** ИНТУРИ́СТ
3 СУВЕНИ́РЫ	**4** КА́ССА

They mean souvenirs, restaurant, cashier, and Intourist. Can you guess which one is which?

1.2 See if you can greet the following people in Russian:

1. Your guide Tamara: say hello, and that you're pleased to meet her.
2. The lady attendant on your corridor: say good afternoon.
3. The hotel receptionist: say good morning.
4. A fellow guest you have had a drink with: say good-bye.

.3 A rather harassed guide is trying to round up a group of visitors. How do they answer his questions? (The first one is done for you.)

1 **Извини́те пожа́луйста, вы ми́стер Наш?** (James Green)
Нет, я ми́стер Грин.
2 **Извини́те пожа́луйста, вы ми́стер Наш?** (Mike Nash)
3 **Извини́те пожа́луйста, вас зову́т Кларк?** (Pat Clarke)
4 **И вас зову́т То́мас?** (Paul Thompson)
5 You are Anna Black—tell the guide your own name.

.4 You and a friend are holding a conversation with the **дежу́рная** on your corridor:

1 First you want the keys for rooms 305, 308, and 310. What numbers do you ask for? (Note that in large hotels, you can get away with using the last two numbers only.)
2 Next you want to know where the bathroom is. What do you say?
3 There doesn't seem to be a towel in your room. What do you ask for?

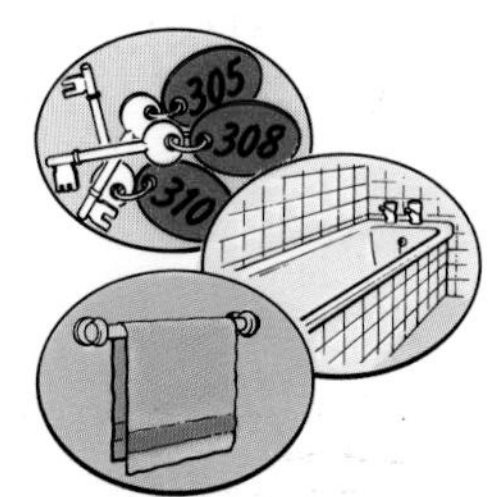

.5 You are looking for the hotel bar and overhear someone explaining where everything is. Can you tell which floor the bar is on? (**Нахо́дится** *nakhoditsa* means "is found/situated"):

Буфе́т нахо́дится на двена́дцатом этаже́.
Бюро́ обслу́живания нахо́дится на четвёртом этаже́.
Бар нахо́дится на пе́рвом этаже́.
Столо́вая нахо́дится на тре́тьем этаже́.

ORDERING DRINKS

Most hotels have a bar (**бар** *bar*) in which you can use foreign currency to buy drinks. Larger ones also have a restaurant (**ресторáн** *ristaran*) and a buffet or snack bar (**буфéт** *boofyet*) where you can get hot and cold drinks and snacks. The snack bar is often self-service, and food such as bread, cold meat, cheese, cucumber, etc., is sold by weight.

Coffee is normally black and rather strong. **Tea** comes without milk, though in large hotels it may be served with lemon. If you want milk, you will have to ask for it. You may also find your tea has been presweetened. There is a variety of syrupy carbonated drinks available in the Soviet Union. It is best to avoid these and go for mineral water (**минерáльная водá** *mineralnaya vada*) or fruit juice (**фруктóвый сок** *frooktoviy sok*).

в буфете/at the buffet

Lucy Brown, a journalist, is on a cultural visit to the Soviet Union. After spending the morning sightseeing, she goes back to the hotel for a drink along with Vadim, the Soviet guide attached to her group. Lucy knows some Russian, and is anxious to practice it.

Vadim: (Shouts to the waitress): Дéвушка! **Дáйте чай, пожáлуйста**. (To Lucy) Что вы хотúте?
Dyevushka! Daitye chai, pazhalasta. Shto vy khatitye?

Lucy: **Ко́фе—с молоко́м.**
Kofi—s malakom.

Waitress: (Writing) Чай, ча́шка ко́фе с молоко́м . . . Э́то всё?
Chai, chashka kofi s malakom . . . Eta vsyo?

Lucy: Да, **э́то всё**. Спаси́бо.
Da, eta vsyo. Spaseeba.

Alice Nash and a friend arrive and sit down at a table.

Waitress: Что вам уго́дно?
Shto vam oogodna?

Alice: **У вас есть пе́пси-ко́ла?**
Oo vas yest Pepsi-Cola?

Waitress: Нет, не́ту. Есть
лимона́д и́ли фрукто́вый сок.
Nyet, neytoo. Yest
limanat ili frooktoviy sok.

Alice: (cheekily) А во́дка у вас есть?
A vodka oo vas yest?

Waitress: (sourly) Нет, у нас во́дки
сего́дня нет!
Nyet, oo nas vodki
sivodnya nyet!

Да́йте чай. Bring me some tea.
де́вушка waitress
Это всё? Is that all?
и/и́ли and/or
у нас сего́дня во́дки нет we have no vodka today

Asking for something to eat or drink

Что вы хоти́те?	*Shto vy khatitye?*	What do you want?
Что вам уго́дно?	*Shto vam oogodna?*	What would you like?
У вас есть пе́пси-ко́ла?	*Oo vas yest Pepsi-Cola?*	Have you got any Pepsi-Cola?
У нас есть фрукто́вый сок.	*Oo nas yest frooktoviy sok.*	We have fruit juice.
Нет, не́ту.	*Nyet, neytoo.*	No, we don't have any.

Горя́чие напи́тки *Hot drinks*

Да́йте ко́фе.	*Daitye kofi.*	Bring me some coffee.
ко́фе с молоко́м/ с са́харом	*kofi s malakom/ s sakharam*	coffee with milk/sugar
чай с лимо́ном/ с мёдсм	*chai s limonam/ s myodam*	tea with lemon/honey
чай без са́хара	*chai byez sakhara*	tea with no sugar

Холо́дные напи́тки *Cold drinks*

молоко́	*malako*	milk
лимона́д	*limanat*	lemon-lime soft drink
байка́л	*baikal*	cola
фа́нта	*fanta*	orange soft drink
минера́льная вода́	*mineralnaya vada*	mineral water
апельси́новый сок	*apilseenaviy sok*	orange juice
я́блочный сок	*yablachniy sok*	apple juice
вишнёвый сок	*vishnyoviy sok*	cherry juice
тома́тный сок	*tamatniy sok*	tomato juice

To say "a cup of coffee," "a glass of tea," "a bottle of lemon-lime soft drink" use these expressions:

ча́шка ко́фе *chashka kofi*
стака́н ча́я *stakan chaya*
буты́лка лимона́да *bootylka limanada*

Of course, you'll need to ask how much it comes to:

Ско́лько с меня́? *Skolka s minya?* How much is that?

the way it works

"The" and "a" (definite and indefinite articles)

There are no articles in Russian, so **ко́фе** *kofi* can mean "coffee," "the coffee," or "a coffee."

How to say: You have

The verb "to have" is not generally used in Russian. Instead, you will hear the expression **у нас** *oo nas* (lit. in the possession of us) for "we have" and **у вас** *oo vas* (lit. in the possession of you) for "you have."

Минера́льная вода́, фрукто́вый сок *(adjectives)*

Adjectives in Russian change depending on the noun they accompany. With masculine nouns, adjectives end in **ый**, **ий**, or **ой**:

но́**вый** бар	*noviy bar*	a new bar
ру́сс**кий** гид	*roosskiy geed*	a Russian guide
больш**о́й** ста́кан	*balshoy stakan*	a large glass

With feminine nouns, adjectives generally end in **ая** (a few end in **яя**):

но́в**ая** ча́шка	*novaya chashka*	a new cup
си́н**яя** буты́лка	*sinyaya bootylka*	a blue bottle

With neuter nouns, adjectives generally end in **ое** (a few end in **ее**):

но́в**ое** окно́	*novaye akno*	a new window
хоро́ш**ее** молоко́	*kharosheye malako*	good milk

Don't worry too much about these different endings. The main part of the word stays the same, and as long as you get this right, you will be able to make yourself understood!

things to do

1.6 **Pronunciation practice**

КОНТО́РА	office	**МУЖСКО́Й**	gentlemen's toilets
ЗВОНО́К	service bell	**ЖЕ́НСКИЙ**	ladies' toilets

1.7 You and your friends are feeling thirsty after an afternoon's sightseeing and go into a cafe.

1. Ask if they have tea with lemon.
2. Ask the waitress to bring you a coffee and an apple juice.
3. Now ask for a bottle of lemon-lime soft drink, and say thank you.

1.8 You and your family go into a buffet for a quick drink before going out to the theater. See if you can talk to the waiter (**официа́нт** *afitseeant*) in Russian:

Waiter: Здра́вствуйте. Что вам уго́дно?
You: (Ask for a cup of coffee and a glass of tea.)
Waiter: Вы хоти́те чай с са́харом или без са́хара?
You: (You want it without sugar.)
Waiter: Без са́хара? Хорошо́. И что еще?*
You: (Ask if there's any tomato juice.)

Waiter: Нет, к сожале́нию (unfortunately). А у нас есть во́дка. Хоти́те во́дку?
You: (Say no thank you. Ask for a fruit juice.)
Waiter: Ну—ко́фе, чай и сок. Э́то всё?
You: (Yes, that's all. Now thank him.)

что ещё? *shto yishcho?* anything else?

ORDERING BREAKFAST

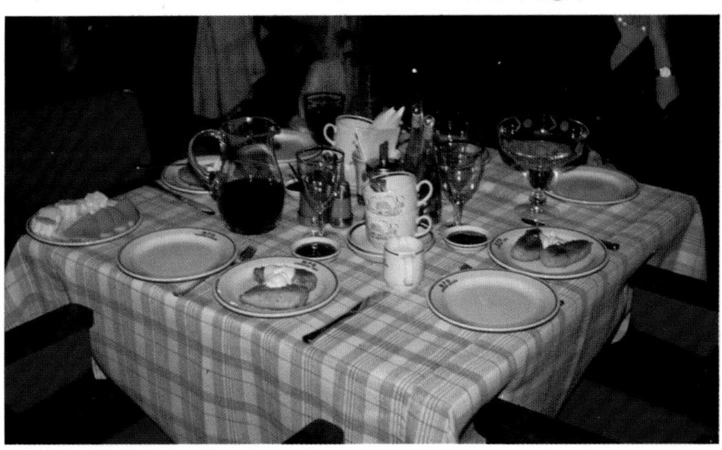

Breakfast is traditionally a fairly substantial meal, served between 8:00 and 10:00 a.m., and although some hotels have now moved over to the Continental breakfast of bread (**хлеб** *khlyep*), rolls and jam (**бу́лочки с варе́ньем** *boolachki s varenyem*), you may also have a choice of hot dishes, cold sliced meats, and cheese. In an old-fashioned hotel you might find smoked fish (**ры́ба** *ryba*) or pancakes with sour cream (**бли́нчики со смета́ной** *blinchiki sa smyetanoi*) or with cottage cheese (**с тво́рогом** *s tvoragam*). Milk products are very popular in the Soviet Union, and **кефи́р** *kefir* (soured milk) is often served at breakfast. A similar drink is **ря́женка** *ryazhenka*. Sour cream is the accompaniment to all kinds of dishes, from soups and stews to pancakes and fruit puddings.

In larger hotels, breakfast may already be laid out on the table, but if there is a choice of hot dishes you may have to ask for what you want.

завтракать/having breakfast

Lucy Brown is having breakfast with Donald Forbes, a retired doctor who learned his Russian in the Air Force. They call the waiter.

Lucy: Молодо́й челове́к!
Maladoi chilavyek!

Waiter: До́брое у́тро. Что вы хоти́те?
Dobraye ootra. Shto vy khatitye?

Lucy: **Я́йца есть?**
Yaitsa yest?

Waiter: Да, коне́чно—у нас омле́т, я́йца всмя́тку, яи́чница с ветчино́й . . .
Da, kanyeshna—oo nas amlyet, yaitsa vsmyatkoo, yaichnitsa s vyetchinoi . . .

Lucy: **Я возьму́ омле́т**.
Ya vazmoo amlyet.

Donald: **Да́йте мне пожа́луйста** бли́нчики со смета́ной.
Daitye mnye pazhalasta blinchiki sa smyetanoi.

Waiter: К сожале́нию у нас бли́нчиков нет. Есть соси́ски и́ли колбаса́.
K sazhalyeniyoo oo nas blinchikav nyet. Yest sasiski ili kalbasa.

Donald: Тогда́ я возьму́ соси́ски.
Tugda ya vazmoo sasiski.

Waiter: Сейча́с. Хоти́те чай и́ли ко́фе?
Syichas. Khatitye chai ili kofi?

Donald & Lucy: Ко́фе, пожа́луйста.
Kofi, pazhalasta.

Молодо́й челове́к!	Waiter! (lit. young man)
сейча́с	at once/right away
коне́чно	of course
тогда́	then
К сожале́нию у нас бли́нчиков нет.	Unfortunately we don't have pancakes.

Что вы хоти́те к за́втраку? ***What do you want for breakfast?***

Я́йца есть?	*Yaitsa yest?*	Are there any eggs?
Сыр есть?	*Syr yest?*	Is there any cheese?
Ка́ша есть?	*Kasha yest?*	Is there any porridge?

Есть омле́т, колбаса́, ветчина́.
Yest amlyet, kalbasa, vyetchina.
There's omelet, (salami-type) sausage, ham.

Есть яи́чница, я́йца всмя́тку/вкруту́ю, соси́ски.
Yest yaichnitsa, yaitsa vsmyatkoo/vkrootuyoo, sasiski.
There are fried eggs*, soft/hard boiled eggs, little sausages.

Я возьму́ бли́нчики со смета́ной. *Ya vazmoo blinchiki sa smyetanoi.*	I'll have pancakes and sour cream.
Я возьму́ соси́ски. *Ya vazmoo sasiski.*	I'll have sausages.
Да́йте мне хлеб, ма́сло, варе́нье. *Daitye mnye khlyep, masla, varenye.*	Give me some bread, butter, jam.
Да́йте мне бу́лочки с варе́ньем. *Daitye mnye boolachki s varenyem.*	Give me some rolls and jam.

*Fried eggs usually come in pairs, and when served with ham may be rather like an omelet.

Language difficulties

Lucy and Donald managed to understand the waiter, but if you are not following what's being said, try one of these:

Повтори́те, пожа́луйста.	*Paftaritye, pazhalasta.*	Please repeat that.
Говори́те ме́дленно.	*Gavaritye myedlinno.*	Speak slowly.
or simply. . .		
Я не понима́ю.	*Ya ni panimayoo.*	I don't understand.

the way it works

Is there?/There is

Есть is a very useful word in Russian. Apart from the infinitive, it is the only form of the verb "to be" that is commonly used, and means "there is . . ./ there are . . ./have you any . . .?" etc.:

Есть молоко́?	*Yest malako?*	Is there any milk?
Да, есть.	*Da, yest.*	Yes, there is.
Есть бу́лочки?	*Yest boolachki?*	Have you got any rolls?
Да, есть.	*Da, yest.*	Yes, we have.

Nouns in the plural

If you are talking about more than one thing, most Russian words take **ы** (or **и** after **г**, **к**, **х**, **ж**, **ч**, **ш**, and **щ**) as their endings:

омле́т	*amlyet*	омле́т**ы**	*amlyety*	omelets
сарди́на	*sardina*	сарди́н**ы**	*sardiny*	sardines
соси́ска	*sasiska*	соси́ск**и**	*sasiski*	sausages
бу́лочка	*boolachka*	бу́лочк**и**	*boolachki*	rolls

Neuter nouns ending in **о** take **а** in the plural:

яйцо́ *yaitso* — я́йца *yaitsa* — eggs

(those ending in **е** take **я** and those ending in **ие** take **ия**)
Note: The adjectives "my" and "your" in the plural are **мои́** *maee* and **ва́ши** *vashi*.

2.1 Here is the breakfast menu at your hotel. You would like fruit juice, fried eggs, rolls with butter and jam, and coffee with milk. Which can you not have?

ГОСТИНИЦА МЕТРОПОЛЬ
Доброе утро!

омлет
сосиски
колбаса

булочки
масло
сыр

напитки
кефир
фруктовый сок
какао

чай с лимоном
кофе чёрный
кофе с молоком

2.2 The waiter is taking orders for breakfast. Tell him what you'd like.

Waiter: До́брое у́тро. Хоти́те яи́чницу, омле́т и́ли соси́ски?
You: (You'll have an omelet.)
Waiter: Омле́т с сы́ром и́ли с ветчино́й?
You: (A ham omelet.)
Waiter: Хорошо́. И что вы хоти́те пить*, чай и́ли ко́фе?
You: (You'll have tea.)

* (to drink)

MAKING PURCHASES 1

Stalls and stands You can buy such things as snacks, drinks, newspapers, and magazines without having to go into a shop. Automatic street vending machines dispense soft drinks, carbonated water (**газиро́вка** *gazirofka*), beer (**пи́во** *piva*), Pepsi-Cola, etc., and kvass (**квас**) — a mildly alcoholic drink made from fermented black bread and malt — is sold from tanks in the street. In summer, Russian beer, which is light and refreshing, can be bought from beer stalls.

You will find stands selling pies (**пирожки́** *pirazhki*), pastries (**пиро́жные** *pirozhnye*), and other snacks, and in Moscow a Russian-American pizza stall is in business. Ice cream (from stalls or ice cream parlors) is extremely popular in summer and winter alike, and there are many varieties to choose from.

You can buy cigarettes (**сигаре́ты** *sigaryety*) and cigars (**сига́ры** *sigary*) from a tobacco stand. Russian-style cigarettes (**папиро́сы** *papirosy*) are thick and very strong, and come complete with cardboard tubes. Newspaper stands sell newspapers, magazines, maps, and guidebooks (look out for the sign **СОЮЗПЕЧА́ТЬ**).

мороженое купить/buying ice cream

Mike Nash and his party have been sightseeing, and have a free half hour before returning to the hotel. Mike wants to find an English paper, but Alice and two of her friends decide to buy some ice cream. They go to an ice cream stall.

Alice: **Ско́лько сто́ит моро́женое?**
Skolko stoit marozhenaye?
Vendor: **Три́дцать и́ли пятьдеся́т копе́ек.**
Tritsat ili pitdisyat kapeyek.
Alice: **Три по́рции по три́дцать, пожа́луйста.**
Tree portsii po tritsat, pazhalasta.

Ско́лько сто́ит моро́женое? How much does an ice cream cost?

в газетном киоске/at the newspaper stand

Assistant: Вы что-нибу́дь хоти́те?
Vy shto-niboot khatitye?
Mike: **У вас есть англи́йская газе́та?**
Oo vas yest angliskaya gazyeta?
Assistant: К сожале́нию нет. Есть америка́нский журна́л.
K sazhalyeniyoo nyet. Yest amerikanskiy zhoornal.
Mike: **Ско́лько он сто́ит?**
Skolka on stoit?
Assistant: Рубль три́дцать копе́ек.
Roobl tritsat kapeyek.
Alice: (running over) **Мне ну́жно купи́ть** ка́рту Ленингра́да.
Mnye noozhna koopeet kartoo Leningrada.
Assistant: Вот ка́рта Ленингра́да. Она́ сто́ит два рубля́ де́сять копе́ек.
Vot karta Leningrada. Ana stoit dva rooblya dyesyat kapeyek.
Alice: **А ско́лько сто́ят откры́тки?**
A skolka stoyat atkrytki?
Assistant: Ка́ждая три́дцать копе́ек.
Kazhdaya tritsat kapeyek.
Alice: **Да́йте мне пять откры́ток**, пожа́луйста.
Daitye mnye pyat atkrytok, pazhalasta.

Вы что́-нибудь хоти́те? Do you want something?
О́чень жаль. I'm very sorry.

ВТОРНИК TUESDAY

How to buy something 1

When you want to buy something, you can say:

У вас есть . . .	*Oo vas yest . . .*	Do you have . . .
англи́йская газе́та?	*angliskaya gazyeta?*	an English newspaper?
Мне ну́жно купи́ть . . .	*Mnye noozhna koopeet . . .*	I need to buy . . .
Я хочу́ . . .	*Ya khachoo . . .*	I want . . .
Я хоте́л бы . . .	*Ya khatyel by . . .*	I'd like . . . (for a man)
Я хоте́ла бы . . .	*Ya khatyela by . . .*	I'd like . . . (for a woman)
моро́женое	*marozhenaye*	an ice cream
америка́нский журна́л	*amerikanskiy zhoornal*	an American magazine
ка́рту Ленингра́да	*kartoo Leningrada*	a map of Leningrad
путеводи́тель	*pootivaditel*	a guidebook

And when you want to know what something costs, say:

Ско́лько сто́ит? *Skolka stoit?* How much does it cost?

Журна́л сто́ит рубль три́дцать копе́ек. *Zhoornal stoit roobl tritsat kapeyek.*	The magazine costs 1 ruble 30 kopecks.
Ка́рта сто́ит два рубля́ де́сять копе́ек. *Karta stoit dva rooblya dyesyat kapeyek.*	The map costs 2 rubles 10 kopecks.
Откры́тки сто́ят три́дцать копе́ек. *Atkrytki stoyat tritsat kapeyek.*	The postcards cost 30 kopecks.
Три по́рции по три́дцать, пожа́луйста. *Tree portsii po tritsat, pazhalasta.*	Three at 30 (kopecks), please.
Да́йте мне пять *Daitye mnye pyat.*	Give me five.

the way it works

I want to buy a map (the accusative case)

When a word is the object of a sentence, and that word is a feminine singular noun, the ending changes:

ка́рт**а** Ленингра́да	*karta Leningrada*	a map of Leningrad
Я хочу́ купи́ть ка́рт**у**.	*Ya khachoo koopeet kartoo.*	I want to buy a map.
англи́йская газе́т**а**	*angliskaya gazyeta*	an English newspaper
Да́йте мне газе́т**у**.	*Daitye mnye gazyetoo.*	Give me a newspaper.

Adjectives in the feminine singular change their endings from **ая** *aya* or **яя** *yaya* to **ую** *uyoo* or **юю** *yooyoo* in the accusative case:

Да́йте америка́нск**ую** газе́т**у**, ру́сск**ую** ка́рт**у**.
Daitye amerikanskuyoo gazyetoo, roosskuyoo kartoo.
Give me an American paper, a Russian map.

Again, don't worry about these endings too much at this stage, as you will be able to make yourself understood even if you don't get them quite right.

things to do

2.3 Can you complete this conversation using the words in the box? Only one word will fit into each of the blanks.

Клиент: До́брый день. У вас есть.............газе́та?
Газетчик: Да. Таймс есть.
Клиент: Ско́лько он............?
Газетчик: ....два́дцать.........
Клиент: Я хочу́ та́кже купи́ть англи́йский...............
Газетчик: О́чень жаль. А у нас есть ....журна́л — Тайм.
Клиент: Да́йте мне..............ка́рту Ленингра́да.
Газетчик: Ка́рта по-ру́сски или по-англи́йски?
Клиент: ....спаси́бо.
Газетчик: Два.............де́сять копе́ек.

рубль	америка́нский	англи́йская
ка́рту	сто́ит	рубля́
журна́л	копе́ек	по-ру́сски

You will find a translation of this dialogue in the key on p. 109. Did you manage to understand it?

2.4 **Ско́лько сто́ит?** How much does it cost?

Practice your numbers by saying how much all these things cost, e.g.:

америка́нский журна́л 1 р. 30 к.

Сто́ит рубль три́дцать копе́ек.

1 ка́рта 2 р. 25 к.

2 ру́сская газе́та 1 р. 10 к.

3 моро́женое 50 к.

4 путеводи́тель 2 р. 5 к.

EATING OUT

Meals Lunch (**обéд** *abyed*) is the main meal in the Soviet Union, and consists of 4 courses — hors d'oeuvre, soup, main course, dessert. It is usually served in hotels and restaurants from 11:30 a.m. to 3:00 or 4:00 p.m. Dinner (**ýжин** *oozhin*) may also have 3 or 4 courses, but you may not be offered soup. It is generally eaten between 7:00 and 10:30 or 11:00 p.m. If you are on a group tour, all your meals may have been arranged for you at your hotel.

The various state-run cafes and snack bars are generally crowded, especially at the end of the working day, and in many of them you eat standing at a counter. A **столóвая** *stalovaya* is the equivalent of a quick cafeteria, and a **буфéт** *boofyet* is a self-service snack bar. You may also come across a **пирожкóвая** *pirazhkovaya* selling mainly pies, a pancake house (**блúнная** *blinnaya*) or a **пельмéнная** *pilmyennaya* specializing in dumplings. There are only a few Western-style cafes in the major cities, but fast food is beginning to catch on in the Soviet Union. A McDonald's restaurant recently opened its doors on Pushkin Square in Moscow, serving a record 30,000 curious people on its first day of business.

The **кафé** *cafe* is really more of a restaurant and serves full meals with drinks,whereas a **ресторáн** *ristaran* is likely to be a more fashionable restaurant where people might go to celebrate an occasion. Many of the best restaurants are in the hotels reserved for foreigners, and some cater to residents only. They may accept Intourist meal vouchers (**обéденные талóны** *abyedenniye talony*) — but you will generally have to reserve in advance.

You will be expected to leave your coat and any bags in the cloakroom. You are not obliged to tip attendants or waiters, as your bill will include a service charge, but most people like to leave a little extra. Most restaurants close at 11:00 or 11:30 at night.

приятного аппетита/bon appétit

Lucy has arranged to interview Tonya, a friend of Vadim's and a rather flamboyant character, for an article she is writing. The three decide to eat out at a well-known restaurant where Vadim has reserved a table.

Vadim: Здра́вствуйте, **я заказа́л стол — на три челове́ка.**
Zdrastvuitye, ya zakazal stol — na tree chilavyeka.

Waiter: Хорошо́. Сюда́, пожа́луйста, сади́тесь. (Handing the menu) Вот меню.
Kharasho. Syooda, pazhalasta, saditycs. Vot minyoo.

Vadim: **Что вы порекоменду́ете** сего́дня?
Shto vy porikamendooitye sivodnya?

Waiter: Ку́рица, она о́чень вку́сная или бефстро́ганов. . .
Kooritsa, ona ochin vkoosnaya, ili befstroganof. . .

Tonya: **О, я о́чень люблю́** бефстро́ганов . . . а шокола́дное моро́женое про́сто пре́лесть!
O, ya ochin looblyoo befstroganof . . . a shakaladnaye marozhenaye prosta pryelist!

Lucy: **Я хоте́ла бы** селёдку, а пото́м ку́рицу.
Ya khatyela by syelyodkoo, a patom kooritsoo.

Vadim: А **я хочу́** сала́т из огурцо́в, и битки́. Скажи́те, Лю́си, вы лю́бите бе́лое и́ли кра́сное вино́?
A ya khachoo salat iz agoortsov, i bitki. Skazhitye, Lucy, vy lyoobitye byelaye ili krasnaye vino?

Lucy:	Бéлое, пожáлуйста.
	Byelaye, pazhalasta.
Tonya:	(interrupting) О, **я предпочитáю** крáсное . . .
	O, ya predpachitayoo krasnaye . . .
Vadim	Вы бýдете слáдкое?
(to Lucy):	*Vy booditye sladkaye?*
Lucy:	**Спаси́бо, не хочý.**
	Spaseeba, ni khachoo.
Waiter:	(Returning) Вы **бýдете закáзывать?**
	Vy booditye zakazyvat?

потóм	then
я óчень люблю́	I love/I'm very fond of
скажи́те	say, tell me

Ресторан Ленинградский
ОБЕДЕННОЕ МЕНЮ

Закуски appetizers
сельдь herring
икра caviar
салат из огурцов cucumber salad

Супы soups
щи cabbage soup/бульон с яйцом clear egg soup
солянка рыбная spicy veg. and fish soup
рассольник vegetable and kidney soup

Горячие блюда hot dishes
курица жареная с картофелем
roast chicken with potatoes
бефстроганов
beef Stroganoff/meatballs with rice
осетрина в томате
sturgeon in tomato sauce

Сладкое dessert
шоколадное мороженое
chocolate ice cream
ромовая баба baba au rum
кисель kissel (type of fruit jelly)

В ресторáне *At the restaurant*

If you have already reserved a table, you can say:

Я заказáл стол.	*Ya zakazal stol.*	I have reserved a table (man speaking).
Я заказáла стол.	*Ya zakazala stol.*	I have reserved a table (woman speaking).

If you haven't, try:

Я хочý стол на два/три/четы́ре человéка. I want a table for 2/3/4 people.
Ya khachoo stol na dva/tree/chityre chilavyeka.

на пять человéк	*na pyat chilavyek*	for 5 people
Это мéсто зáнято?	*Eta myesta zanyata?*	Is this place taken?

The waiter will say:

Сюдá, пожáлуйста, сади́тесь. This way, please, sit down.
Syooda, pazhalasta, sadityes.

or

Жаль, все местá зáняты. I'm sorry, we're full up (lit. all the places are occupied).
Zhal, vsye myesta zanyaty.

You might like to ask the waiter:

Да́йте мне меню́, пожа́луйста. *Daitye mnye minyoo, pazhalasta.*	Give me the menu, please
Что вы порекоменду́ете сего́дня? *Shto vy porikamendooitye sivodnya?*	What do you recommend today?
Принеси́те нам буты́лку вина́. *Prinesitye nam bootylkoo vina.*	Bring us a bottle of wine.
Ещё оди́н/одна́/одно́ . . . , пожа́луйста. *Yishcho adin/adna/adno . . . , pazhalasta.*	Another . . . , please.
Бо́льше ничего́. *Bolshe nichevo.*	Nothing else.
Где здесь туале́т? *Gdye zdyes twalyet?*	Where is the toilet?
Да́йте счёт, пожа́луйста. *Daitye schot, pazhalasta.*	Bring the bill, please.

and the waiter might say:

Вы бу́дете сла́дкое/ко́фе? *Vy booditye sladkaye/kofi?*	Are you having dessert/coffee?
Вы бу́дете зака́зывать? *Vy booditye zakazyvat?*	Would you like to order?
Сейча́с принесу́. *Syichas prinesoo.*	I'll bring it at once.
К сожале́нию, э́того у нас сего́дня нет. *K sazhaleniyoo, etava oo nas sivodnya nyet.*	I'm sorry, we have none today.
Заплати́те в ка́ссу. *Zaplatitye v kassoo.*	Pay the cashier.

Likes and dislikes

Я о́чень люблю́ бефстро́ганов. *Ya ochin looblyoo befstroganof.*	I love beef Stroganoff.
Это про́сто пре́лесть! *Eta prosta pryelist!*	It's simply delightful!
Вы лю́бите бе́лое и́ли кра́сное вино́? *Vy lyoobitye byelaye ili krasnaye vino?*	Do you like white or red wine?
Я предпочита́ю кра́сное. *Ya predpachitayoo krasnaye.*	I prefer red.
Э́то о́чень вку́сно. *Eta ochin vkoosna.*	It's very tasty.

▶▶▶ **What to order** The Soviet Union is not noted for its cooking, but there are still one or two good restaurants to be found. Appetizers are often filling, and the first course (**пе́рвое** *pyervaye*) can be the most interesting. Be sure to try the smoked or pickled fish, red or black caviar (**кра́сная и́ли чёрная икра́** *krasnaya ili chornaye ikra*) and pancakes (**блины́** *bliny*). Another favorite is **столи́чный сала́т** *stalichniy salat*, a salad of mixed vegetables in mayonnaise. Soups are also very good, and include varieties of the well-known borsch (**борщ**) — beet soup, usually containing pieces of meat and other vegetables; shchi (**щи**) — cabbage soup; and salianka (**соля́нка**) — a very filling spiced vegetable soup with either smoked fish or meat. Fish dishes to try are those with sturgeon (**осетри́на** *asietrina*), pike-perch (**суда́к** *sudak*), and salmon (**сёмга** *syomga* or **лососи́на** *lasasina*).

Favorite meat dishes include of course beef stroganoff (**бефстро́ганов**); goulash (**гуля́ш**); chicken Pojarsky (**котле́ты пожа́рские**); chicken "tabaka" (**цыплёнок «табака́»** *tsyplyonok tabaka*) — in which the chicken is split, flattened, and roasted with garlic; and chicken Kiev (**котле́ты по-ки́евски**). Popular dishes on Russian menus are kebabs (**шашлы́к**), schnitzel (**шни́цель**), beefsteak (**бифште́кс**), and pilaff (**плов** *plof*). Meat dishes generally come with assorted vegetables (**гарни́р** *garnir*). Ice creams and fruit compote (**компо́т**) are the most common desserts, but there are also various cakes (**то́рты** *torty*), pies (**пироги́** *piragi*), and puddings (**пу́динги** *poodingi*).

For a full list of food, see p. 114. See also the section on shopping, pp.67–69.

За ва́ше здоро́вье! ***Your good health!***

You will want to try some Russian wine with your meal, and perhaps to propose a few toasts in the Russian fashion. Ask for a bottle of white, red, or rosé wine — **буты́лку бе́лого/кра́сного/ро́зового вина́** *(bootylkoo byelava/krasnava/rozovava vina)*, and say whether you want it dry, sweet, or sparkling — **сухо́е/сла́дкое/шипу́чее** *(sukhoye/sladkaye/shipoocheye)*. Russians tend to prefer their wines sweet. You might also want one of the following:

beer (dark/light)	**пи́во (чёрное/све́тлое)**	*piva (chornaye/svyetlaye)*
champagne	**шампа́нское**	*shampanskaye*
whisky	**ви́ски**	*viski*
cognac	**конья́к**	*kanyak*
gin and tonic	**джин с то́ником**	*dzhin s tonikam*
vodka	**во́дка**	*vodka*
liqueur	**ликёр**	*likyor*

ВТОРНИК TUESDAY

the way it works

More nouns

Nouns ending in a soft sign can be either masculine or feminine:

лосо́сь (masc.) salmon **форе́ль** (fem.) trout

These nouns drop the soft sign and take **и** in the plural: лосо́с**и**.

More about adjectives

Adjectives in the plural end in **ые** or **ие**:

холо́дная заку́ска *khalodnaya zakooska*	a cold appetizer	холо́дн**ые** заку́ск**и** *khalodnye zakooski*	cold appetizers
горя́чее блю́до *garyacheye blyooda*	a hot dish	горя́ч**ие** блю́д**а** *garyachiye blyooda*	hot dishes

When the adjective comes after a noun, the endings **ый**, etc., **ая**, **ое**, and **ые** are shortened. For example **вку́сный** (tasty):

бефстро́нагов вку́сен*	*befstroganof fkoosen*
ку́рица вкусн**а́**	*kooritsa fkoosna*
моро́женое вку́сн**о**	*marozhenaye fkoosna*
битки́ вку́сн**ы**	*bitki fkoosny*

*Note the insertion of **е** to make pronunciation easier.

The form ending in **о** is used all the time to mean "it's . . . ," e.g.:

Жа́рк**о**.	*Zharka.*	It's hot.
Хо́лодн**о**.	*Kholadna.*	It's cold.
Великоле́пн**о**.	*Velikalyepna.*	It's wonderful.
Ужа́сн**о**.	*Oozhasna.*	It's awful.

Russian case endings and pronouns

You will probably have realized that the endings of many words depend on where the word is placed in the sentence. This is because there are six different "cases" in Russian. We have already seen the accusative case, which is used when a word is the object of the sentence. The dative case is used when we would generally use the word "to" in English, and also after certain prepositions.

This is how it works for the pronouns we have seen so far:

nominative			*accusative*			*dative*		
I	**я**	*ya*	me	**меня́**	*minya*	(to) me	**мне**	*mnye*
you	**вы**	*vy*	you	**вас**	*vas*	(to) you	**вам**	*vam*
we	**мы**	*my*	us	**нас**	*nas*	(to) us	**нам**	*nam*

Here are some examples:

I see you.	Я ви́жу **вас**.	*Ya vizhoo vas.*
I give (to) you.	Я даю́ **вам**.	*Ya dayoo vam.*

things to do

5 **Pronunciation practice** You may come across one of these when looking for somewhere to eat. Can you pronounce them?

КАФЕ́-МОРО́ЖЕНОЕ	ice-cream parlor
ШАШЛЫ́ЧНАЯ	kebab house
ЗАКУ́СОЧНАЯ	snack bar

6 Lucy is with a group of friends at a restaurant, and is the only person who speaks Russian. What does she order for everyone?

red caviar, lamb with rice, compote
cabbage soup, chicken Kiev, vanilla (**вани́льное**) ice cream
tomato salad (**из помидо́ров**), goulash with potatoes, cheese
sturgeon, pork with mushrooms (**с греба́ми**), kissel

Now her friends would like some drinks, so Lucy asks the waiter for the following: a bottle of red wine, a bottle of white wine, a gin and tonic, a light beer, and a vodka.

LONG-DISTANCE TRAVEL

▶▶▶ **Trains** The Russian railways are very geared up to long-distance travel, and a long journey can be an exhilarating experience. Tourists transferring from one major city to another often make the journey overnight in a comfortable sleeper (**спáльный вагóн** *spalniy vagon*). This can have either two berths (more comfortable and more expensive) or more usually four, with men and women sharing the same compartment — men usually take a turn in the corridor while ladies are dressing or undressing! Your ticket will include bed linen, blankets, and a pillow. There is no first or second class, and the old "hard" and "soft" categories have now disappeared, along with the wooden seats. Compartments can be **междунарóдный** *mizhdoonarodniy* (international — the most comfortable), **купéйный** *koopeiniy* (generally 4-berthed) or **óбщий** *obshchiy* (general). **Плацкáртный** *platskartniy* is a cheaper seat in a reserved coach.

If you are traveling independently, be sure to book ahead, and if you are going to be traveling for several days, it's a good idea to take some food and drink with you. Most trains have a dining car (**вагóн-рестóрáн** *vagon-ristaran*) and for a few kopecks, the corridor attendant (**проводнúк** *pravadnik*) will bring glasses of tea at regular intervals. He or she will also wake you at a specific time if asked.

на поезде/on the train

The group with which Lucy is traveling has made the overnight journey from Leningrad and is due to arrive in Moscow early in the morning. Lucy engages in conversation with a Russian lady in her compartment.

Passenger: Извини́те пожа́луйста, **мо́жно откры́ть окно́?**
Izvinitye pazhalasta, mozhna atkryt akno?

Lucy: (whispering) Пожа́луйста. Скажи́те, **в кото́ром часу́ по́езд прихо́дит** в Москву́?
Pazhalasta. Skazhitye, v katoram chasoo poyizd prikhodit v Maskvoo?

Passenger: Я не зна́ю то́чно . . . в семь часо́в, ду́маю.
Ya ni znayoo tochna . . . v syem chasof, doomayoo.

Lucy: Спаси́бо. Вы живёте в Москве́?
Spaseeba. Vy zhivyotye v Maskve?

Passenger: Нет, в Заго́рске. **Мне ну́жно де́лать переса́дку в** Москве́. **По́езд на Заго́рск отхо́дит в** полови́не деся́того. Заго́рск о́чень краси́вый го́род . . .
Nyet, v Zagorski. Mnye noozhna dyelat pirisatkoo v Maskve. Poyizd na Zagorsk atkhodit v palavinye disyatava. Zagorsk ochin krasiviy gorat . . .

Male passenger: (grumbling) Прошу́ вас не беспоко́ить меня́. . . пять часо́в утра́!
Prashoo vas ni bespakoit minya. . . pyat chasof ootra!

Мо́жно откры́ть окно́?	Can I open the window?
Я не зна́ю то́чно.	I don't know exactly.
ду́маю	I think
Вы живёте в Москве́?	Do you live in Moscow?
краси́вый го́род	a beautiful town
Прошу́ вас не беспоко́ить меня́.	Please (I ask you) don't disturb me.
пять часов утра	5 o'clock in the morning

Asking about train times

В кото́ром часу́ . . .? Когда́ . . .? (At) what time . . .? (lit. In what hour?) When . . .?
V katoram chasoo? Kugda?
В кото́ром часу́ прихо́дит по́езд в Москву́? What time does the train arrive in Moscow?
V katoram chasoo prikhodit poyizd v Maskvoo?
Когда́ отхо́дит по́езд на Заго́рск? When does the train leave for Zagorsk?
Kugda atkhodit poyizd na Zagorsk?
сле́дующий по́езд/после́дний по́езд the next train/the last train
sliduyooschiy poyizd/paslyedniy poyizd
в полови́не деся́того at half past nine
v palavini disyatava

В биле́тной ка́ссе *At the ticket office*

Ско́лько сто́ит биле́т в . . .? How much is a ticket to . . .?
Skolka stoit bilyet v . . .?
биле́т туда́ и обра́тно round-trip ticket
bilyet tooda i abratna
биле́т в оди́н коне́ц one-way ticket
bilyet v adin kanyets
Мне ну́жно де́лать переса́дку? Do I need to change?
Mnye noozhna dyelat pirisatkoo?
Это прямо́й по́езд It's a direct train.
Eta pryamoi poyizd.
Бу́дет переса́дка в Ха́рькове. You have to change at Kharkov.
Boodyet pirisatka v Kharkovi.
С како́й платфо́рмы? — Платфо́рма но́мер два. From which platform? — Platform no. 2.
S kakoi platformy? — Platforma nomir dva.

На вокза́ле *At the station*

ПРИБЫ́ТИЕ arrival
pribytiye
ОТПРАВЛЕ́НИЕ departure
atpravlyeniye
расписа́ние поездо́в train schedule
raspisaniye payizdof
спра́вочное бюро́ information office
spravachnaye byooro
зал ожида́ния waiting room
zal azhidaniya
ка́мера хране́ния багажа́ baggage room
kamira khranyeniya bagazha
бюро́ нахо́док lost and found
byooro nakhodak

На поезде *On the train*

Это место занято?	*Eta myesta zanyata?*	Is this seat taken?
Нет, это свободно.	*Nyet, eta svabodna.*	No, it's free.

Место *myesta* is a seat on a train, and **спальное место** *spalnoye myesta* is a place in a sleeping compartment. The word for compartment is **купе** *coopay*. You may find yourself in a smoking compartment (**вагон для курящих** *vagon dlya kuryashchikh*). If you want a nonsmoking compartment, look for a **вагон для некурящих** *vagon dlya nikuryashchikh* or the sign **не курить** *ni kooreet* (no smoking).

Можно . . .? *Can I/May I . . .?*

This is a very useful word in Russian, and you use it when you want to ask someone's permission to do something. For example:

Можно открыть окно? *Mozhna atkryt akno?* — Can I open the window?

Можно закрыть дверь? *Mozhna zakryt dver?* — Can I close the door?
Можно курить? *Mozhna kooreet?* — Do you mind if I smoke?
Можно включить радио? *Mozhna fkloochit radeeo?* — Can I turn on the radio?
Можно выключить свет? *Mozhna vykloochit svyet?* — Can I turn out the light?

If the anwer is "no, you can't," use **нельзя** *nilzya:*

Нельзя курить. *Nilzya kooreet.* — You mustn't smoke.

Где вы живёте? *Where do you live?*

Вы живёте в Москве? *Vy zhivyotye v Maskve?* — Do you live in Moscow?
Я живу в Загорске. *Ya zhivoo v Zagorski.* — I live in Zagorsk.
Вы живёте в Нью-Йорке? *Vy zhivyotye v Nyoo Yorki?* — Do you live in New York?
Я живу в Лондоне. *Ya zhivoo v Londani.* — I live in London.

See p. 112 for all the forms of **жить** *zhit* (to live).

TELLING THE TIME

Котóрый час? ***What time is it?***

When traveling by public transportation, it is useful to be able to tell the time. In Russian, it works like this:

Час. *Chas.*	It's 1 o'clock.
Два/три/четы́ре/ часá. *Dva/tree/chitirye chasa.*	It's 2/3/4 o'clock.
Пять часóв. *Pyat chasof.*	It's 5 o'clock.
дéсять минýт шестóго *dyeasyat minoot shistova*	ten past five
чéтверть шестóго *chetvyert shistova*	quarter past five
двáдцать пять минýт шестóго *dvatsat pyat minoot shistova*	twenty-five past five
полови́на шестóго *palavina shistova*	half past five

What you are saying literally is "ten minutes of the sixth," "a quarter of the sixth," "half of the sixth," etc. Note that **шестóго** is pronounced as though the **г** was a **в**; this is true for all words ending in **-ого/-его** (**трéтий** takes the ending **-его**). After the half hour, the pattern changes, and you use **без** *byez* (minus), and the cardinal number for the hour:

без двадцати́ шесть	*byez dvatsati shest*	twenty to six
без чéтверти шесть	*byez chetvyerti shest*	quarter to six
без пяти́ шесть	*byez pyati shest*	five to six
шесть часóв	*shest chasof*	six o'clock
утрá/дня/вéчера	*ootra/dnya/vyechera*	in the morning/afternoon/ evening

For "at," use **в: в шесть часóв** at 6 o'clock.

For train times, opening and closing times of museums, shops, etc., the 24-hour clock is often used, so you may see

13:00 (or 13 ч.)	тринáдцать часóв
15:30	пятнáдцать часóв три́дцать минýт

Don't worry if you can't cope with expressing the time yourself — just listen for those numbers (minutes and hours). If you don't understand, ask the person to repeat it:

Пожáлуйста, ещё раз. *Pazhalasta, yishcho raz.* Once more, please.

If you still can't catch it, ask for it to be written down:

Напиши́те, пожáлуйста. *Napishitye, pazhalasta.* Please write it down.

в аэропорту/at the airport

Air travel Owning to the long distances between cities in the Soviet Union, it is just as common to travel by air as by train, and fares are not expensive. Airports, however, can be extremely crowded and you may have to face long lines. Airports are often some distance away from a town, with transfer by coach or car. Flight attendants hand out candy and give helpful pre-flight information—however this probably won't be English, and you may find that once the plane has taken off, the flight attendant is no longer on board! There are no separate areas for nonsmokers on board Soviet airplanes.

The vocabulary of flying

Когда́ отлета́ет пе́рвый самолёт в Москву́ *Kugda atlitayet pyerviy samalyot v Maskvoo?* — When is the first flight to Moscow?

В семь часо́в. *V syem chasof.* — At seven o'clock.

Э́то рейс но́мер сто три́дцать в Ки́ев? *Eta reiss nomir sto tritsat v Kiev?* — Is this flight number 130 to Kiev?

стюарде́сса	*stewardyessa*	flight attendant
регистра́ция багажа́	*rigistratsiya bagazha*	luggage check-in
вход на поса́дку	*vkhod na pasatkoo*	departure gate
поса́дка	*pasatka*	stopover, transit

the way it works

Verbs and how they work

You have seen quite a few Russian verbs now, in various forms. The ending **-ть** means "to . . . ," e.g., **кури́ть** *kooreet* (to smoke), **сто́ить** *stoit* (to cost), **заказывать** *zakazyvat* (to order). This part of the verb is called the infinitive. There are two verb conjugations in Russian, a first, or **-е-** conjugation, and a second, or **-и-** conjugation. Here is an example of a first conjugation verb:

понима́ть ***panimat*** to understand

я понима́ю *ya panimayoo*	I understand	мы понима́ем *my panimayem*	we understand
ты* понима́ешь *ty panimayesh*	you understand	вы понима́ете *vy panimayetye*	you understand
он понима́ет *on panimayet*	he/it understands	они понима́ют *ani panimayoot*	they understand
она понима́ет *ana panimayet*	she/it understands		
оно понима́ет *ano panimayet*	it understands		

***ты** is the familiar form of "you," used when speaking to close friends, children, and animals. You may hear it, but you aren't likely to need it.

Here is an example of a second, or **-и-**, conjugation verb:

говори́ть *gavareet* to speak, say

я говор**ю́** *ya gavaryoo*	I speak	мы говор**и́м** *my gavarim*	we speak
ты говор**и́шь** *ty gavarish*	you speak	вы говор**и́те** *vy gavaritye*	you speak
он, она́, оно́ говор**и́т** *on, ana, ano gavarit*	he, she, it speaks	они́ говор**я́т** *ani gavaryat*	they speak

For a list of common Russian verbs, see p. 112.

I live in Moscow (the locative case)

The locative case is so called because it's used when you're talking about the place where something is located. (It is also known as the "prepositional," as it is only used after prepositions.) After **в** *v* (in, at, to) or **на** *na* (on, at, to) nouns take the locative endings. Most take the ending **е** (those ending in -**ия** and -**ие** change to -**ии**, and feminine nouns ending in a soft sign change to -**и**):

Заго́рск—краси́вый го́род. *Zagorsk—krasivy gorat.*	Zagorsk is a lovely town.
Я живу́ **в** Заго́рске. *Ya zhivoo v Zagorski.*	I live **in** Zagorsk.
Москва—столи́ца Росси́и. *Maskva—stalitsa Rassii.*	Moscow's the capital of Russia.
Мы **в** Москве́. *My v Maskve.*	We're **in** Moscow.

Verbs of motion

If you are going *to* a place and there is movement involved, the prepositions **в** and **на** are followed by nouns in the accusative case (i.e., the ending **а** changes to **у** for feminine singular nouns):

По́езд прихо́дит **в** Москв**у́**.	The train *arrives* in Moscow.
По́езд отхо́дит на Ленингра́д.	The train *leaves* for Leningrad.

things to do

3.1 **Pronunciation practice** Here are some signs you will see at the station, and in many other places in the Soviet Union. Can you pronounce them?

ВХОД (entrance) **ВЫХОД** (exit)
ЗАПАСНОЙ ВЫХОД (emergency exit)
ВХОДА НЕТ (no entrance) **ВЫХОДА НЕТ** (no exit)

.2 You have an hour's wait before your train departs and want to sit down. What do you look for?

1 ка́мера хране́ния
2 спа́льный ваго́н
3 зал ожида́ния
4 бюро́ нахо́док

.3 Tonya wants to get to Moscow. She asks the assistant in the information office to look at the schedule. Can you answer her questions?

То́ня спра́шивает: (asks)

В кото́ром часу́ отхо́дит пе́рвый по́езд на Москву́?
В кото́ром часу́ прихо́дит по́езд в Москву́?
Когда́ отхо́дит после́дний по́езд из (from) Ленингра́да?
Это прямо́й по́езд, или бу́дет переса́дка?

РАСПИСАНИЕ ПОЕЗДОВ – ЛЕНИНГРАД-МОСКВА

поезд номер	отправление	прибытие
25	0.30	12·30
12	10.00	22.00
3	17.40	05.50

.4 Счастли́вого пути́! *Schastlivava pooti!* (Have a good trip!)

You have made it to the train, and you're looking for a seat. Can you communicate with your fellow passengers?

You: (Ask if this seat is taken.)
Passenger: Нет, свобо́дно.
You: (It's very stuffy—ask if you can open the window.)
Passenger: Пожа́луйста.
You: (You forgot to look at the schedule. Ask what time the train arrives in Kiev.)
Passenger: В Ки́ев? Часо́в в оди́ннадцать.
You: (You're feeling hungry. Ask where the dining car is.)
Passenger: Это ря́дом! (next door)

.5 **Кото́рый час?** The Soviet Union stretches across eleven time zones. Can you say what time it is in different places? E.g.:

London 3:15. — В Ло́ндоне че́тверть четвёртого
Leningrad 6:15 — В Ленингра́де, че́тверть седьмо́го

1 London: 12:30 — Moscow: 3:30
2 Moscow: 11:15 — Irkutsk: 16:15
3 New York: 5:00 — Leningrad: 13:00
4 Yalta: 6:45 — Tashkent: 8:45

ASKING FOR DIRECTIONS

Out and about in Leningrad There are many museums, churches, and interesting places to see in Leningrad, the great northern city built on water. If you are staying here, be sure to visit the Peter and Paul Fortress, which stretches along the north bank of the River Neva. Built by Peter the Great, founder of Leningrad, it contains the Peter and Paul Cathedral in which the tsar himself is buried. Across the river is **St. Isaac's Cathedral** (**Исáакиевский собóр** *Isakievskiy sabor*), with its splendid golden dome, built in the style of St. Peter's in Rome. Visitors can climb up to the top for a magnificent view across the city. Worth visiting also is the **Kazan Cathedral** (**Казáнский собóр** *Kazanskiy sabor*), now the Museum of the History of Religion and Atheism.

The **Winter Palace** (**Зи́мний Дворéц** *Zimniy Dvaryets*), well known for its impressive blue and white facade, was once the home of the tsars, but now houses the world famous **Hermitage Museum** (**Эрмитáж** *Ermitazh*), so vast you would need six months to do it justice. The museum is particularly notable for its collection of French Impressionist and post-Impressionist paintings, and the many works of Picasso. Other museums are the Russian Museum, the Lenin Museum, and the Museum of Literary History.

как пройти в ...?/how do I get to ...?

It is their last afternoon in Leningrad, and Mike Nash and the members of his party are scattered in various parts of the city.

Alice wants to get to Palace Square. She asks a passerby for directions.

Alice: Извините пожа́луйста, **где** Дворцо́вая **пло́щадь?**
Izvinitye pazhalasta, gdye Dvartsovaya ploshchad?

Passerby: Э́то недалеко́. Иди́те пря́мо, пото́м напра́во.
Eta nidalyeko. Iditye pryama, patom naprava.

недалеко́ not far **напра́во** (to the) right

Next, she is looking for the Hotel Astoria.

Alice: **Как пройти в гости́ницу** «Асто́рия»?
Kak praeetee v gastinitsoo Astoriya?

Passerby: Асто́рия? — вон там, на углу́!
Astoriya? — von tam, na oogloo!

на углу́ on the corner

Meanwhile, Mike is trying to find the way to the Finland Station.

Mike: **Как пройти́ на** Финля́ндский **вокза́л?**
Kak praeetee na Finlyandskiy vagzal?

Passerby: Напра́во, зате́м нале́во. Вы сра́зу уви́дите его сле́ва.
Naprava, zatyem nalyeva. Vy srazoo ooviditye yevo slyeva.

зате́м then **нале́во** (to the) left **сра́зу** at once, right away

Shopping and the arts Visitors to Leningrad should not miss taking a stroll down the **Nevsky Prospekt** (**Не́вский проспе́кт**), the city's most famous boulevard, with its many shops, churches, and cinemas. And for entertainment there's the **Kirov Theater** (**Теа́тр и́мени Ки́рова** *Tiatr imyeni Kirava*), home of the Kirov ballet, opera, and orchestra companies. Leningrad also has its own "White Nights" arts festival, which is held every year in the third week of June.

Alice decides to pay a visit to the "Gastiny Dvor," the famous department store on the Nevsky Prospekt. She shows a passerby her map.

Alice: Скажи́те пожа́луйста, **где нахо́дится** Гости́ный Двор?
Skazhite pazhalasta, gdye nakhoditsa Gastiny Dvor?
Passerby: Мы на Садо́вой у́лице, а Гости́ный Двор там. Иди́те пря́мо, пото́м нале́во.
My na Sadovoi oolitse, a Gastiniy Dvor tam. Iditye pryama, patom nalyeva.

Мы на Садо́вой у́лице. We're on Garden Street.

It's getting late, so Lena decides to take a taxi to the theater.

Lena: **Мо́жно?** (she gets in)
Mozhna?
Driver: Куда́ вам?
Kooda vam?
Lena: **В теа́тр** и́мени Ки́рова—**скоре́е**.
V tiatre imyeni Kirava—skaryeye.
Driver: Хорошо́, пое́хали!
Kharasho, payekhali!

бы́стро quickly
пое́хали let's go!

Указа́ния ***Directions***

It's fairly straightforward asking for directions in Russian. You can just ask **Где . . .?** (Where's . . .?) — or you can say **Где нахо́дится . . .?** (Where's . . . situated?):

Где Дворцо́вая пло́щадь? *Gdye Dvartsovaya ploshchad?*	Where's Palace Square?
Где Эрмита́ж? *Gdye Ermitazh?*	Where's the Hermitage?
Где нахо́дится Гости́ный Двор? *Gdye nakhoditsa Gastiniy Dvor?*	Where's Gastiny Dvor?
Где нахо́дится Иса́акиевский собо́р? *Gdye nakhoditsa Isakievskiy sabor?*	Where's St. Isaac's Cathedral?

Как пройти́ в/на means "how do I get to" if you are going somewhere on foot:

Как пройти́ в гости́ницу «Асто́рия»? *Kak praeetee v gastinitsoo Astoriya?*	How do I get to the Hotel Astoria?
Как пройти́ на Финля́ндский вокза́л? *Kak praeetee na Finlyandskiy vagzal?*	How do I get to the Finland Station?

If you need to use some form of transportation, say **Как проéхать?** *Kak prayekhat?* instead. Of course, you will need to be able to understand the reply. This is what you can expect to hear:

Вот он/онá/онó *Vot on/ana/ano.*	There it is.
Э́то (не) далекó. *Eta (ni) dalyeko.*	It's (not) far.
Иди́те пря́мо/обрáтно, потóм напрáво/нале́во. *Iditye pryama/abratna, patom naprava/nalyeva.*	Go straight ahead/back, then right/left.
Вон там, на углу́/напрóтив/ря́дом. *Von tam, na ooglu/naprotiv/ryadam.*	It's over there, on the corner/opposite/ next door.
Вы срáзу уви́дите егó/её, нале́во. *Vy srazoo ooviditye yevo/yeyo, nalyevo.*	You'll see it at once, on the left.

Кудá? means "Where to?" If you decide to take a taxi, the driver might say:

Кудá вам? *Kooda vam?* Where do you want to go?

and you might reply:

В теáтр и́мени Ки́рова, скорéе! *V tiatr imyeni Kirava, skaryeye!*	To the Kirov Theater, and quickly!

Я иду́ в теáтр *I'm going to the theater*

Я иду́ в гости́ницу «Астóрия».	I'm going to the Hotel Astoria.
в теáтр и́мени Ки́рова.	to the Kirov theater.
в ресторáн «Невá».	to the Neva restaurant.
Я иду́ на Héвский проспéкт.	I'm going to the Nevsky Prospekt.
на Финля́ндский вокзáл.	to the Finland Station.
на Дворцóвую плóщадь.	to Palace Square.

the way it works

Let's go to . . .

The verb to use when going somewhere on foot is **идти***

я иду́	*ya idoo*	I go	**мы идём**	*my idyom*	we go
ты идёшь	*ty idyosh*	you go	**вы идёте**	*vy idyote*	you go
он/онá/онó идёт	*on/ana/ano idyot*	he, etc., goes	**они́ иду́т**	*ani idoot*	they go

*Note that a few verbs have infinitives ending in **-ти.**

If someone is telling you which way to go, you'll hear **Иди́те** . . . *Iditye* (You go . . .), and if a suggestion is being made, it's **Пойдём (в . . .)** *Paeedyom v* (Let's go to . . .). When your guide feels it's time to make a move, he or she might say **Пошли́**! *Pashli* (Let's go!), and if you're in a taxi or a bus, the driver will say **Поéхали!** *Payekhali!*

В *and* на

Both of these can mean "to," and it's a question of knowing which to use. There were quite a few examples in the dialogues — here are some more:

Пойдём . . . Let's go . . .

в кинó	*v kino*	to the movie theater
в цирк	*v tsirk*	to the circus
в музéй	*v moozei*	to the museum
в кафé	*v kafe*	to the cafe
на стадиóн	*na stadion*	to the stadium
на пóчту	*na pochtoo*	to the post office
на вы́ставку	*na vystavkoo*	to the exhibition
на стáнцию метрó	*na stantsiyoo mitro*	to the subway

Егó *and* её

For "him" or "it" referring to a masculine or neuter noun in the accusative case, use **его** *yevo*, for "her" or "it" referring to a feminine noun, use **её** *yeyo*:

Вот собóр — я ви́жу егó.	There's the cathedral — I see it.
Вот гости́ница — я ви́жу её.	There's the hotel — I see it.
Вот Лéна — я очéнь её люблю́.	There's Lena — I like her very much!

Егó and **её** are also used for "his" and "her":

егó рóдина *yevo rodina* his country **её гóрод** *yeyo gorat* her town

things to do

3.6 **Pronunciation practice** You will see these street signs all over the Soviet Union. See if you can guess their English equivalents:

СТÓЙТЕ ИДИ́ТЕ СТÓП ПЕРЕХÓД БЕРЕГИ́СЬ АВТОМОБИ́ЛЯ

3.7 Finding your way around

(a) You have a free afternoon and want to look around the town. Find different ways of asking how to get to

1 the movie theater **2** the hotel **3** the stadium

(b) You are standing outside the hotel (see the map on p. 44), and hear your Russian guide giving these directions to some tourists. Can you tell where each of them wants to go?

1 Иди́те пря́мо, налéво, потóм напрáво. Вы уви́дите егó напрáво.
2 Э́то недалеко. Иди́те напрáво, на Большóй проспéкт, и вы уви́дите её на углу́.
3 Вон там, напрóтив, ря́дом с теáтром.

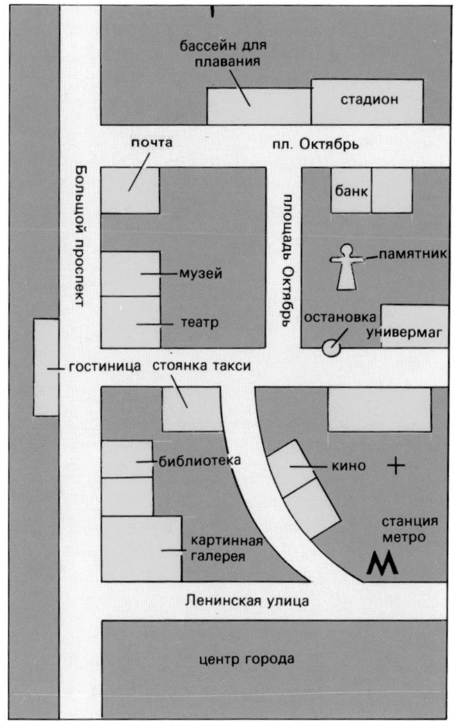

банк	bank
бассе́йн для пла́вания	swimming pool
библиоте́ка	library
гости́ница	hotel
карти́нная галере́я	art gallery
кино́	movie theater
музе́й	museum
остано́вка	bus stop
по́чта	post office
собо́р	cathedral
стадио́н	stadium
ста́нция метро́	subway
теа́тр	theater
универма́г	dept. store
це́нтр го́рода	center of town
це́рковь	church
у́лица	street
стоя́нка такси́	taxi stand

.8 You and various members of your group have asked the way to the Hotel Rossiya, the Chekhov Museum, and Revolution Square, and you hope you have followed the directions correctly — but have you? Read the signs, and say where you actually ended up.

TRANSPORTATION IN THE CITY

The Metro There are subway systems in Moscow, Leningrad, Kiev, Minsk, and Tashkent, but the most famous one is in Moscow. Any visit to the capital is not complete without a trip on the Metro (indicated by the letter M, illuminated at night), with its fast, efficient service and its clean and beautifully decorated stations, many of which rival museums with their decor of marble, bronze, mosaics, and glass. Visit **Пло́щадь Револю́ции** *Ploshchad Revalyootsii* for its "Heroes of the Revolution" — 40 pairs of bronze statues, **Комсомо́льская** *Komsomolskaya* for its marble, mosaics, and chandeliers, and **Новослобо́дская** *Novoslabodskaya* for its stained glass.

If you are to cope with traveling on the Metro, the main thing is to be able to decipher the names of stations (written, of course, in Cyrillic script). Exits, entrances, interchange stations, and directions are well signed — but only in Russian. When you have spotted your station, see what color line it's on, work out whether you need to change anywhere (**де́лать переса́дку**) to get onto that line, and the rest is easy. You pay a flat fare of 5 kopecks, which you drop into a slot at the top of the escalator. The red light changes, and you pass through the barrier — there are no tickets involved. If you don't have 5 kopecks, there are change machines (**размéн** *razmyen*), and you can also change money at the **кáсса**. The name of every station, plus the one following it, is announced on arrival, so listen for the stop you want. The Metro is open from 6:00 a.m. to 1:00 a.m. (5:00 a.m. to 2:00 a.m. on some public holidays), and there are fast trains every few minutes. It is best to avoid the rush hours (7:00 to 9:00 a.m. and 4:00 to 6:30 p.m.).

ПЕРЕХОД

Алис едет на метро/Alice takes the Metro

Mike and Alice Nash and the other members of their student group have also arrived in Moscow. Alice and her friend Sergei are anxious to see the Metro, and break away from the rest.

Alice is looking for the station "Sportivnaya," but can't locate it on her map. She asks for help.

Alice: Извинúте, **вы не знáете где стáнция** «Спортúвная»?
Izvinitye, vy ni znayitye gdye stantsiya Spartivnaya?

Traveler: Вам нужнá крáсная лúния. Вот схéма Метрó — и вот Спортúвная.
Vam noozhna krasnaya liniya. Vot skhema Mitro — i vot Spartivnaya.

Alice: **Мне нáдо дéлать пересáдку?**
Mnye nada dyelat pirisatkoo?

Traveler: Нет, не нýжно.
Nyet, ni noozhna.

вы не знáете где..? do you know where . . .?
схéма Метрó plan of the metro

ЧЕТВЕРГ THURSDAY

Sergei went in a different direction, and now he is trying to get back to the Prospekt Marx. However, he isn't sure he's on the right train:

Sergei: Извини́те, **э́тот по́езд идёт до ста́нции** «Проспе́кт Ма́ркса»?
Izvinitye, etat poyizd idyot do stantsii Praspekt Marksa?

Traveler: Да, идёт.
Da, idyot.

Sergei: Вы мне ска́жете, когда́ я до́лжен сходи́ть?
Vy mnye skazhitye, kugda ya dolzhen skhadit?

Traveler: Това́рищ, Проспе́кт Ма́ркса — сле́дующая ста́нция!
Tavarishch, Praspekt Marksa — slyeduyooshchaya stantsiya!

Вы мне ска́жете, когда́ я до́лжен сходи́ть? Will you tell me when I have to get off?

Я схожу́. I'm getting off.

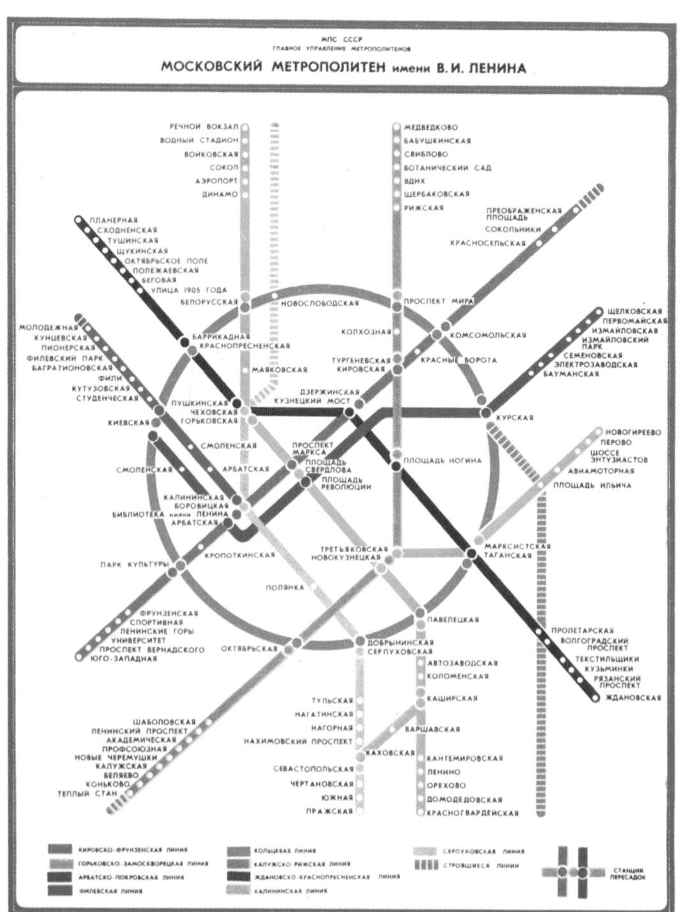

Making inquiries

Какóй *kakoi* (what/which?) is a useful word when asking questions. It works like any other adjective:

Какáя лúния для . . .? *Kakaya liniya dlya . . .?*	Which line for . . .?
Какáя слéдующая стáнция . . .? *Kakaya slyeduyooshchaya stantsiya?*	What's the next station?

Note also:

На какóй лúнии?	*Na kakoi linii?*	On which line?
на крáсной лúнии	*na krasnoi linii*	on the red line
на калúнинской лúнии	*na kalininskoi linii*	on the Kalinin line

Э́тот пóезд идёт до стáнции «Проспéкт Мáркса». This train is going to
Etat poyizd idyot do stantsii Praspekt Marksa. Prospekt Marx.

When you're on the train, listen for these announcements:

Осторóжно, двéри закрывáются! *Astarozhna, dveri zakryvayootsa!*	Attention, doors closing!
Слéдующая — Проспéкт Мáркса. *Slyeduyooshchaya — Praspekt Marksa.*	Next stop, Prospekt Marx.

I need to, I must

You have already encountered the expression **нýжно** *noozhna*:

Мне надо дéлать пересáдку?	**— Нет, вам не нýжно.**
Do I need to change?	— No, you don't need to.

A similar expression that you'll hear frequently is **вам нáдо** *vam nada* meaning "you ought to." **Не нáдо** *ni nada* on its own is often used with the meaning "you don't have to" or simply "don't!"

Дóлжен *dolzhen* means "must" or "have to," but is used in a more specific way. It is rather like a short adjective:

Sergei:	**Я дóлжен сходúть.**	*Ya dolzhen skhadit.*	I have to get out.
Alice:	**Я должнá сходúть.**	*Ya dulzhna skhadit.*	I have to get out.
Traveler:	**Вы должны́ сходúть.**	*Vy dulzhny skhadit.*	You must get out.

Цветá *Tsveta* (Colors)

It's useful to know your colors so you can make sure that you're on the right line:

black	**чёрный**	*chorniy*	purple	**пурпýрный**	*poorpoorniy*
white	**бéлый**	*byeliy*	mauve	**сирéневый**	*siryeneviy*
red	**крáсный**	*krasniy*	orange	**орáнжевый**	*aranzheviy*
blue (dark)	**сúний**	*siniy*	pink	**рóзовый**	*rozaviy*
(light)	**голубóй**	*galooboi*	gray	**сéрый**	*syeriy*
green	**зелёный**	*zilyoniy*			
yellow	**жёлтый**	*zholtiy*	dark	**тёмный**	*tyomniy*
brown	**корúчневый**	*karichneviy*	light	**свéтлый**	*svyetliy*

Buses and streetcars If you're feeling really adventurous, you can try taking the bus (**автóбус** *aftoboos*), trolley (**троллéйбус** *trallyeiboos*) or streetcar (**трамвáй** *tramvai*). A flat-rate fare operates here too, but you put your money in a collecting box and tear a ticket from the roll hanging up. If you don't have the correct amount, wait until you have gotten some change from another passenger before taking your ticket. If the bus is crowded, you will find people passing their fares along to the person nearest the box. Tickets should be validated at one of the stamping machines inside the bus. Both buses and streetcars run from very early in the morning (5:00 or 5:30 a.m.) to 1:00 a.m.

Где останóвка автóбуса? *Gdye astanofka aftoboosa?*	Where's the bus stop?
останóвка троллéйбуса/трамвáя *astanofka trallyeiboosa/tramvaya*	trolley/streetcar stop
Вам нýжно нóмер 12. *Vam noozhna nomir dvyenatsat.*	You need a number 12.
В центр гóрода, какóй нóмер? *V tsentr gorada, kakoi nomir?*	What number for the town center?

Taxis can be found at taxi stands (**стоя́нка таксú** *stayanka taksi*), recognizable by the sign of a large T, and can also be hailed in the street (though this is not always successful). Russian taxis have a checked stripe either along the side or on the roof, and an illuminated light in the windshield or on the roof indicates that the taxi is free. All taxis are metered, and you do not pay anything extra for additional passengers or for luggage. If you know in advance that you're going to need a taxi, ask your hotel service bureau to call one for you.

На вокзáл, пожáлуйста.	*Na vagzal, pazhalasta.*	To the station, please.
В аэропóрт . . .	*V aeroport . . .*	To the airport . . .
Я спешý!	*Ya spishoo!*	I'm in a hurry!

DRIVING

Renting a car It is now possible to rent a car (**взять напрокáт машúну** *vzyat naprakat mashinoo*) for driving around town or on recognized Intourist routes, though this facility exists only in a few major towns. In others, you car comes complete with a driver. Be prepared to reserve the car well in advance (ask at your hotel), and be especially alert when driving in the city. Roads are often very wide and lanes are not clearly marked. The speed limit is 60 kph (37 mph) in town, 90 kph (56 mph) elsewhere. It is advisable to stick to these limits, not least because road surfaces can suddenly deteriorate. Main country roads are generally two-lane roads with no median strip, but highways are few and those that exist do not conform to Western standards.

Drive on the right side, and do not cross an unbroken single or double centerline. Priority is to the right, and streetcars and buses come before cars, so give them a wide berth. Seat belts are compulsory for drivers and front seat passengers. Road signs are international, and parking is generally not too much of a problem in the Soviet Union. Drinking and driving is not permitted.

If you are involved in an accident, contact your nearest Intourist Office (**бюрó Интурúста** *byooro Intoorista*) immediately.

Мне нужнá машúна. *Mnye noozhna mashina.*	I need a car.
Мне нýжно заказáть машúну. *Mnye noozhna zakazat mashinoo.*	I need to order a car.
Где я могý остáвить машúну? *Gdye ya magoo astavit mashinoo?*	Where can I park?

Gasoline comes in liters:

Три́дцать ли́тров, пожа́луйста. *Tritsat litraf, pazhalasta.* 30 liters, please.

You will find these words connected with driving useful:

доро́га *daroga*	road	**води́тельские права́** *vadityelskiye prava*	driver's license
маршру́т *marshroot*	route	**перекрёсток** *pirikryostok*	crossroads
шоссе́ *shassay*	main road	**запра́вочная ста́нция** *zapravachnaya stantsiya*	service station
автодоро́га *aftodaroga*	highway	**ма́сло и вода́** *masla i vada*	oil and water
светофо́р *svyetafor*	traffic lights	**милиционе́р** *militsianyer*	policeman

For a list of car parts, see p. 114.

Road signs

ДЕРЖИ́ТЕСЬ ПРА́ВОЙ СТОРОНЫ́	Keep to the right
ВЪЕЗД ЗАПРЕЩЁН	No entry
СТОЯ́НКА ЗАПРЕЩЕНА́	No stopping
ОДНОСТОРО́ННЕЕ ДВИЖЕ́НИЕ	One-way traffic
ОБЪЕ́ЗД	Detour
ОПА́СНО	Danger

the way it works

Taking the subway

The verb to use when you're going by some form of transportation is **ехать** *yekhat* (to go):

я е́ду	*ya yedoo*	I go
ты е́дешь	*ty yedish*	you go
он/она́ е́дет	*on/ana yedit*	he/she goes
мы е́дем	*my yedim*	we go
вы е́дете	*vy yeditye*	you go
они́ е́дут	*ani yedoot*	they go

Я **е́ду** на по́езде	I go by train
на маши́не	by car
на такси́	by taxi
А́лис **е́дет** на Метро́	Alice goes by Metro
на трамва́е	by streetcar
на тролле́йбусе	by trolley

Note however that if it's the actual train, car, etc., you're talking about, then you use **идти́**: По́езд **идёт** бы́стро *Poyizd idyot bystra* (The train is going fast).

Talking about possessions (the genitive case)

(a) The group's luggage; the luggage of the group: When we say "'s" or "of the" in English, in Russian there is a special case — the possessive or genitive case. Masculine and neuter nouns take an **-а** (those ending in **й**, a soft sign, or **е** take **я**) and feminine nouns lose their ending in **-а** and take **-ы** (or **-и** for those ending in **-я**, a soft sign, or after **г**, **к**, **х**, **ж**, **ч**, **ш**, and **щ**).

Vadim's trip	Поéздка Вади́**ма**	*Payezdka Vadima*
Lena's watch	Часы́ Лé**ны**	*Chasy Lyeny*

Adjectives in the genitive case drop their normal endings and take **-ого/-его** (*-ovo/-yevo*) with masculine and neuter nouns, **-ой/-ей** (*-oi/-yei*) with feminine nouns. Again, you will hear all these different endings, but don't worry too much about getting them right yourself.

(b) The genitive case is used after certain prepositions. Here are some of them: **для** *dlya* (for); **до** *do* (to, up to, as far as, before); **из** *iz* (from, out of); **от** *ot* (from); **без** *byez* (without). It is also used when telling the time (see p. 35).

Я éду до стáн**ции** Университéт.	I'm going to "University" station.
Э́тот пóезд прихóдит из Москв**ы́**.	This train comes from Moscow.

Pronouns in the genitive case are the same as in the accusative case: **меня**, **тебя**, **его** (**него** after a preposition), **её** (**неё** after a preposition), **нас**, **вас**, **их** (**них** after a preposition):

Э́то для **меня**? — Да, э́то для **вас**.	Is it for me? — Yes, it's for you.

things to do

1 **Pronunciation practice** It is important to be able to read the names of stations when traveling on the Metro; here are some of the places you may want to go to:

КИ́ЕВСКАЯ	АРБА́ТСКАЯ	КРОПО́ТКИНСКАЯ
БИБЛИОТЕ́КА	И́МЕНИ ЛЕ́НИНА	ПЛО́ЩАДЬ СВЕРДЛО́ВА

Here are three more signs you will see when traveling by Metro. What do you think they mean?

ОПУСТИ́ТЕ* 5 КОПЕ́ЕК　　К ПОЕЗДА́М　　ВЫ́ХОД В ГО́РОД

*__опусти́ть__ *apoostit* to lower

4.2 You are peering at a Russian map and trying to figure out where everything is. See if you can match the items below with the appropriate signs:

(*a*) остано́вка авто́буса
(*b*) запра́вочная ста́нция
(*c*) ста́нция метро́
(*d*) светофо́р
(*e*) стоя́нка такси́

4

1

2

3

5

4.3 Now you should be able to make yourself understood on all forms of transportation. Here's the test!

1 You need to get back to your hotel, but can't see the Metro station. What do you ask a passerby?
2 You're on the Metro and looking for the station Prospekt Mira. Can you ask a fellow traveler where it is on the map?
3 You decide to take a trolley. Can you ask a passerby where the stop is?
4 You're in a taxi. Ask the driver to take you to the theater.
5 You're at a service station and need some gasoline (**бензи́н** *benzeen*). Ask for 40 liters.

MUSEUMS AND ENTERTAINMENT

Out and about in Moscow Whether you are on a tour, or have time off during a business trip, a visit to the **Kremlin (Кремль** *Kreml*) — Moscow's ancient walled citadel — is a must. From Red Square, where the fairy-tale cathedral of St. Basil (**храм Васи́лия Блаже́нного** *khram Vasiliya Blazhennava*) attracts visitors worldwide, the main entrance, for official visitors only, is the gate by the famous Spassky clock tower (**Спа́сская ба́шня** *Spasskaya bashnya*) — one of 20 such towers along the Kremlin walls. The public entrance to the Kremlin is the Trinity Gate. Once inside, you will see the Belfry of Ivan the Great, the tallest of the Kremlin buildings, with the enormous Tsar's Bell (**Ца́рь ко́локол** *Tsar kolakol*) at its foot. There are several splendid gold-domed churches inside the Kremlin walls, among them the Assumption Cathedral (**Успе́нский собо́р** *Oospenskiy sabor*) where coronations once took place, the Annunciation Cathedral (**Благове́щенский собо́р** *Blagaveshchenskiy sabor*) where the tsars attended services, and the Cathedral of the Archangel Michael (**Арха́нгельский собо́р** *Arkhangilskiy sabor*) where you can see many of their tombs, including that of Ivan the Terrible. These cathedrals are open to the public, but tickets must be bought first from the cashier in the Trinity Gardens.

Anyone can stroll around the Kremlin complex between dawn and dusk, but not all buildings are open to the public. Of those that are, however, the most fascinating for its contents is without doubt the Armory (**Оруже́йная пала́та** *Oroozheinaya palata*). Now a museum, it contains among other things the coaches, jewels, crowns, and thrones of the tsars, and the magnificent costumes of Catherine the Great.

▶▶▶ **Museum opening times** vary considerably, so it is worth checking first, but most open around 10 a.m. and close at 6 or 7 p.m. Many museums are closed on Mondays (some on Tuesdays) as well as the first or last day of the month for cleaning, but are open all day Sunday. Museums are closed on public holidays. There is usually a small entrance charge, and you will have to leave coats, bags, and cameras in the cloakroom.

в музее/at the museum

It is late afternoon, and Donald decides he's just got time to visit another museum before returning to the hotel. He finds his way successfully, but he's not sure what time the museum closes, so he asks at the ticket window (**ка́сса**).

Donald: Прости́те, **в кото́ром часу́ закрыва́ется музе́й?**
Prastitye, v katoram chasoo zakryvaitsa moozei?

Cashier: В во́семь часо́в.
V vosyem chasof.

Donald: Отли́чно. **Да́йте оди́н биле́т**, пожа́луйста — и **катало́г**.
Atlichna. Daitye adin bilyet, pazhalasta — i katalok.

Cashier: Извини́те, здесь нельзя́ фотографи́ровать. На́до оста́вить аппара́т в гардеро́бе.
Izvinitye, zdyes nilzya fatagrafiravat. Nada astavit apparat v gardirobye.

прости́те excuse me **отли́чно** excellent

Visiting a museum or gallery

Когда́ открыва́ется галере́я? When does the gallery open?
Kugda atkryvaitsa galereya?

В кото́ром часу́ закрыва́ется музе́й? What time does the museum close?
V katoram chasoo zakryvaitsa moozei?

Оди́н биле́т, пожа́луйста. *Adin bilyet, pazhalasta.*	One ticket, please.
Да́йте мне/ско́лько сто́ит katoло́г? *Daitye mnye/skolka stoit katalok?*	Give me/how much is a catalog?
На́до оста́вить аппара́т в гардеро́бе. *Nada astavit apparat v gardirobye.*	You have to leave your camera in the cloakroom.

Planning an outing Most Russians book tickets for theaters, concerts, etc., well ahead, and tickets for the really popular venues such as the Bolshoi Theater (**Большо́й теа́тр**), the Conservatory of Music (**Консервато́рия** *Conservatoriya*), the modern theaters Sovrimyenik (**Совреме́нник**) and Taganka (**Теа́тр на Тага́нке** *Tiatr na Taganki*) are hard to come by if you have not reserved in advance. Your hotel service bureau may be able to obtain tickets for you, or you can try through Intourist. Failing that, you can go to the theater itself and see if you can get in because of last-minute cancellations.

Theater and concert performances usually start at 7:00 or 7:30 p.m. (there may be a Sunday matinee at 12:00). After the usher has torn off the **контро́ль** *kantrol* part of your ticket, deposit your coat, umbrella, etc., in the cloakroom (**гардеро́б** *gardirob*) and pick up a cloakroom ticket (**номеро́к** *namirok*). You'll probably be asked if you want to rent binoculars (**бино́кль ну́жен?** *binokl noozhen?*) for a small fee. You'll probably want a program (**програ́мма**) and if you're not sure where you're sitting, ask: **Где моё ме́сто?** *Gdye mayo myesta?*

что вам хочется посмотреть?/what would you like to see?

Lucy decides she would like to go to the ballet or to a concert if she can manage to get a ticket. She discusses it with Vadim.

Lucy: Я о́чень хочу́ пойти́ на бале́т и́ли на конце́рт сего́дня ве́чером, и́ли мо́жет быть посмотре́ть ру́сский фильм.
Ya ochin khachoo paeetee na balyet ili na kantsert sivodnya vyecheram, ili mozhet byt pasmatryet roosskiy film.

(Vadim picks up *Leisure in Moscow* and scans the pages)

Vadim: Посмо́трим . . . В Ма́лом теа́тре идёт «Дя́дя Ва́ня», пье́са Че́хова, в Большо́м теа́тре даю́т бале́т «Жизе́ль», и во Дворце́ съе́здов игра́ет Моско́вский Госуда́рственный Орке́стр. Вы лю́бите му́зыку?
Pasmotrim . . . V Malam tiatri idyot "Dyadya Vanya," pyesa Chekhava, v Balshom tiatri dayoot balyet "Zhizel," i va Dvartse syezdaf igrayet Maskovskiy Gasoodarstvinniy Arkestr. Vy lyoobitye moozykoo?

Lucy: Да, о́чень люблю́!
Da, ochin lyooblyoo.

мо́жет быть	perhaps	**посмо́трим**	let's see
пье́са Че́хова	a play by Chekhov	**му́зыка**	music

Что идёт сего́дня ве́чером в теа́тре? *What's playing at the theater this evening?*

Я о́чень хочу́ пойти́ . . . — I'd love to go . . .
Ya ochin khachoo paeetee . . .

в теа́тр/кино́/на бале́т — to the theater/movie theater/ballet
v tiatr/v kino/na balyet

в о́перу/на конце́рт — to the opera/a concert
v opiroo/na kantsert

посмотре́ть фи́льм/пье́су — to see a film/play
pasmatryet film/pyesoo

«Дя́дя Ва́ня» идёт в Ма́лом теа́тре.
"Dyadya Vanya" idyot v Malam tiatri.
Uncle Vanya is playing at the Maly Theater.

Даю́т бале́т «Жизе́ль» в Большо́м теа́тре.
Dayoot balyet "Zhizel" v Balshom tiatri.
They're performing the ballet *Giselle* at the Bolshoi Theater.

Моско́вкий Госуда́рственный Орке́стр игра́ет . . .
Maskovskiy Gasoodarstvyenniy Arkestr igrayet . . .
The Moscow State Orchestra is playing . . .

. . . в Кремлёвском Дворце́ съёздов
. . .v Krimlyovskam Dvartse syezdaf
. . . at the Kremlin Palace of Congresses

в театральной кассе/at the theater box office

Lucy wants to try her luck at the Bolshoi Theater, so she and Donald rush off to see if they can get tickets:

Lucy: **Два биле́та на сего́дня**, пожа́луйста, на «Жизе́ль».
Dva bilyeta na sivodnya, pazhalasta, na "Zhizel."

Cashier: На сего́дня все биле́ты про́даны. У меня́ оста́лось то́лько три-четы́ре ме́ста на за́втра.
Na sivodnya vsye bilyety prodany. Oo minya astalas tolka tri-chitirye myesta na zaftra.

все биле́ты про́даны all the tickets are sold

Disappointed, they go to the concert hall to see if they can get seats. They line up by a sign saying "**Прода́жа биле́тов на сего́дня**" *(Tickets for today's performance).*

Lucy: **У вас есть биле́ты на сего́дняшний конце́рт?**
Oo vas yest bilyety na sivodnyashniy kantsert?

Cashier: Да, есть. Вы хоти́те на балко́н и́ли в амфитеа́тр?
Da, yest. Vy khatitye na balkon ili v amfitiatr?

Lucy: **Два ме́ста на балко́не**, пожа́луйста.
Dva myesta na balkone, pazhalasta.

Cashier: Вот они́ — пя́тый ряд, пра́вая сторона́.
Vot ani — pyatiy ryad, pravaya starana.

Lucy: Скажи́те, **когда́ начина́ется конце́рт?**
Skazhitye, kugda nachinaitsa kantsert?

Cashier: В семь часо́в, через два́дцать мину́т. Вы пришли́ как раз во́время!
V syem chasof, chiryez dvatsat minoot.
Vy prishli kak raz vovremya!

ряд, сторона́ row, side **че́рез два́дцать мину́т** in 20 minutes
Вы пришли́ как раз во́время! You have come just in time!

Buying a ticket

два биле́та на сего́дня/на за́втра/на вто́рник *dva bilyeta na sivodnya/na zaftra/na ftornik*	2 tickets for today/ tomorrow/Tuesday
два ме́ста на «Жизе́ль»/на «Руса́лку» *dva myesta na "Zhizel"/na "Roosalkoo"*	2 seats for *Giselle*/for *Rusalka*
У вас есть биле́ты на сего́дняшний конце́рт? *Oo vas yest bilyety na sivodnyashniy kantsert?*	Do you have any tickets for today's concert?
Все биле́ты про́даны. *Vsye bilyety prodany.*	All the tickets are sold.
У меня́ оста́лось то́лько три-четы́ре ме́ста на за́втра. *Oo minya astalas tolka tri-chitirye myesta na zaftra.*	I have only 3 or 4 seats for tomorrow.
на второ́е ию́ня/на пе́рвое февраля́ *na ftaroye iyoonya/na pyervaye fivralya*	for 2nd June/for 1st February
Вы хоти́те балко́н и́ли амфитеа́тр? *Vy khatitye balkon ili amfitiatr?*	Do you want balcony or ground floor?
на балко́не, на бельэтаже́ *na balkoni, na byeletazhé*	in the balcony, dress circle
. . . в парте́ре *. . . v parteri*	. . . in the stalls
ряд пя́тый, пра́вая/ле́вая сторона́ *ryad pyatiy, pravaya/lyevaya starana*	row 5, right/left side
Когда́ начина́ется конце́рт/представле́ние? *Kugda nachinaitsa kantsert/pridstavlyeniye?*	When does the concert/ performance begin?
Нача́ло в девятна́дцать часо́в, цена́ три рубля́ пятьдеся́т коп. *Nachala v divyatnatsat chasof, tsena tree rooblya pitdisyat kop.*	It starts at 7 p.m., price 3 r. 50 k.

Look on your ticket and you'll see which part of the auditorium you're sitting in:

ло́жа	a box
орке́стр	orchestra pit
парте́р	stalls
амфитеа́тр	ground floor
балко́н	balcony
бельэта́ж	dress circle
пе́рвый я́рус	first circle
второ́й я́рус	second circle
галере́я	gallery

You will also see the date, the time the performance starts, your row and seat number, and whether it's on the right, left, or in the middle (**середи́на** *siridina*). For dates, see p.113.

If your Russian is not up to a play or a film, you can always go to the circus (**цирк** *tsirk*), or to a musical at the Stanislavsky and Nemirovich-Danchenko Musical Theater, to an operetta at the Operetta Theater (**Моско́вский теа́тр опере́тты** *Maskovskiy tiatr opiretty*) or to a show at the Puppet Theater (**Центра́льный теа́тр ку́кол** *Tsintralniy tiatr kookal*).

the way it works

Reflexive verbs

You may have noticed that some verbs end in **ся** or **сь**. These are called reflexive verbs (the verb reflects the action of the speaker, and the ending **ся** can often be translated by "self"). Many verbs can be either reflexive or non-reflexive, e.g., **открыва́ть** to open, **открыва́ться** to be open (lit. open itself).

Reflexive verbs ending in **-аться** take these endings:

-а́юсь	-а́емся
-а́ешься	-а́етесь
-а́ется	-а́ются

В Большом театре *At the Bolshoi . . .*

Большóй (*balshoi*) and **мáлый** (*maly*) are adjectives meaning "large" and "small" (though the more usual adjective for small is **мáленький** *malinkiy*). Adjectives in the locative case (i.e., after **в** or **на** when there is no movement involved) end in

-ом/-ем for masculine and neuter nouns:	в Мáл**ом** теáтре (at the Little Theater)
-ой/-ей for feminine nouns:	на Крáсн**ой** плóщади (in Red Square)

Весь *Vyes All*

This is an adjective, and it occurs in all sorts of useful expressions:

весь день (masc.)	*vyes dyen*	all day
всю недéлю* (fem.)	*vsyoo nidyelyoo*	all week
всё врéмя (neuter)	*vsyo vreymya*	all the time
все лю́ди (plural)	*vsye lyoodi*	all people

Всё on its own in the neuter form means "all," "everything" (and sometimes "all the time").

*Expressions of time are often in the accusative case — the nominative case in the feminine is **вся** *vsya* (**недéля** *nidyelya* = week).

Expressions of time

вчерá	*fchera*	yesterday
сегóдня у́тром	*sivodnya ootram*	this morning
сегóдня вéчером	*sivodnya vyecheram*	this evening
зáвтра нóчью	*zaftra nochyoo*	tomorrow night
на прóшлой недéле	*na proshloi nidyeli*	last week
на бу́дущей нéделе	*na boodooshchei nidyeli*	next week

things to do

4.4 **Pronunciation practice** You'll probably see these signs at plays or films. Pronounce them correctly, and say what you think they mean:

.5

Центральный Музей Исскуства

Музей открыт с $9.^{00}$ до $20.^{00}$, касса работает до $19.^{30}$ ч.
Выходной день: понедельник
Санитарный день: последний день каждого месяца.

1 If you wanted to visit this museum on a Tuesday, would you be able to get in?
2 You have an hour to spare before meeting a friend at 8 o'clock. Would it be a good idea to go to the museum?
3 Apart from the last day of the month, at what other times is the museum closed?

.6 1 For what date is this ticket valid?
2 In what part of the theater would you be sitting, and on what side?
3 What row and seat number?

БОЛЬШОЙ ТЕАТР
Б/кн. №. четверг 13 июня 1989 года
000735 вечер БЕЛЬЭТАЖ левая сторона
ряд 8 место 5
цена 2 р. 30 к.

.7 You are the only person in your group who speaks Russian, and have been persuaded to make inquiries at the ticket office on behalf of your friends. How would you cope with their requests?

1 Ian and Hilary want two tickets in the balcony for tomorrow.
2 Judy wants to know what time the performance starts.
3 Elizabeth wants a ticket in the stalls — in the middle — for this evening.
4 James and Sarah want to know if there are any seats for today's concert.
5 The cashier only has tickets for February 7. What does she say?

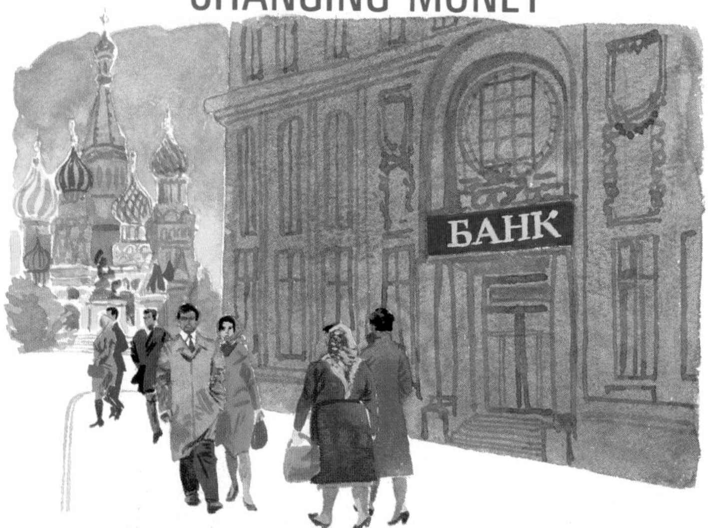

By far the easiest way to change money (**де́ньги** *dyengi*) is simply to go to your hotel currency exchange desk (**обме́н де́нег** *abmyen dyenek*). You will need the currency declaration you filled out at customs, and you will be given a receipt (**квита́нция** *kvitantsiya*) for the transaction. You can also change money at airports and banks (banking hours are approximately 9:30 a.m. to 12:30 p.m. from Monday to Friday). Traveler's checks and foreign currency can be used in Intourist hotels and restaurants and in the hard currency shops reserved for foreigners.

The Russian **ruble** (**рубль** *roobl*, pl. **рубли́** *roobli*) is divided into 100 **kopecks** (**копе́йка** *kapyeika*, pl. **копе́йки** *kapyeiki*). Rubles come in bills of up to 100 r., and there is a silver-colored 1-ruble coin. Kopecks are either silver or copper coins.

мне надо обменять деньги/I need to change some money

Mike Nash and his group of students plan to spend the day shopping, but Mike realizes he is running short of money. He goes to the hotel exchange bureau.

Mike: **Здесь мо́жно разменя́ть доро́жные че́ки?**
Zdyes mozhna razminyat darozhniye cheki?

Clerk: **Да, мо́жно.**
Da, mozhna.

Mike: **Я** та́кже **хочу́ обменя́ть англи́йскую валю́ту** — де́сять фу́нтов.
Ya takzhe khachoo abminyat angliskuyoo valyootoo — dyesyat foontaf.

Clerk: Да́йте ваш па́спорт, пожа́луйста, и ва́шу* деклара́цию.
Daitye vash paspart, pazhalasta, i vashoo diklaratsiyoo.

(Mike hands over the documents)

Тепе́рь распиши́тесь . . . Пожа́луйста, вот вам се́мьдесят рубле́й, и квита́нция.
Tipyer raspishityes . . . Pazhalasta, vot vam syemdisyat rooblei i kvitantsiya.

Mike: А па́спорт где?
A paspart gdye?

Clerk: Извини́те ми́стер Наш — вот он.
Izvinitye mister Nash — vot on.

***Ва́шу** is the accusative form of **Ва́ша**.

Changing money

Где ближа́йший банк/Госба́нк/обме́н де́нег? *Gdye blizhaishiy bank/Gosbank/abmyen dyenek?*	Where's the nearest bank/ State bank/currency exchange?
Мо́жно разменя́ть доро́жные че́ки? *Mozhna razminyat darozhnye cheki?*	Can I change traveler's checks?
. . . обменя́ть англи́йскую валю́ту? *. . . abminyat angliskuyoo valyootoo?*	. . . change some English currency?
. . . америка́нские до́ллары/англи́йские фу́нты *. . . amerikanskiye dollary/angliskiye foonty*	. . . American dollars/ English pounds
Како́й сего́дня курс? *Kakoi sivodnya koors?*	What's the exchange rate today?
Ско́лько вам ну́жно? *Skolka vam noozhna?*	How much do you need?
де́сять фу́нтов/два́дцать до́лларов *dyesyat foontaf/dvatsat dollaraf*	ten pounds/twenty dollars
Распиши́тесь — вот три́дцать рубле́й, и квита́нция. *Raspishityes — vot tritsat rooblyei, i kvitantsiya.*	Sign here — here's 30 rubles and your receipt.

the way it works

Recognizing the genitive plural; numbers and money

You have probably noticed the ending **-ов** (sometimes **-ев**) in expressions such as **шесть часóв** (six o'clock). This is one of the genitive plural endings in Russian. The genitive plural is always used after numbers from five upwards. This is how many nouns behave in the genitive plural:

masculine	*neuter*	*feminine*
пять фýнто**в**	дéсять мест	вóсемь газéт
pyat foontaf	*dyesyat myest*	*vosyem gazyet*
five pounds	ten places	eight papers
(adds **-ов**)	(drops the **-о**)	(drops the **-а**)

Nouns ending in **е** or a soft sign take **-ей** in the genitive plural:

двáдцать площад**éй** *dvatsat plashchadyei* twenty squares

The number 1 takes the nominative singular, but numbers 2, 3, and 4 are followed by the genitive singular in Russian. This is how it works for money:

оди́н рубль *adin roobl*	1 ruble	одн**á** копéйк**а** *adna kapyeika*	1 kopeck
три рубл**я́** *tree rooblya*	3 rubles	три копéйк**и** *tree kapyeiki*	3 kopecks
шесть рубл**éй** *shest rooblyei*	6 rubles	шесть копé**ек** *shest kapeyek*	6 kopecks

It's complicated, but don't worry! For money you'll soon recognize these expressions, and generally speaking you can avoid using different endings for numbers by saying or pointing to what you want, then giving the number, e.g.:

бýлочка — пять, пожáлуйста roll — 5, please
boolachka — pyat, pazhalasta
морóженое — три, пожáлуйста ice cream — 3, please
marozhenaye — tree, pazhalasta

things to do

5.1 You are running short of cash, so you go to the currency exchange bureau in your hotel.

1 Ask if you can change some American dollars.
2 Ask if you can change £25.
3 See if it's possible to change traveler's checks.
4 Ask what the exchange rate is today.

5.2 You go into a bank to change money, and the clerk says to you: **Да́йте ва́шу деклара́цию, пожа́луйста**. Does he want:

(*a*) your receipt
(*b*) your currency declaration form
(*c*) your traveler's checks?

5.3 You go over to the cashier with your chit, and the cashier says: **Вот вам со́рок пять рубле́й два́дцать копе́ек**. Is he giving you:

(*a*) 25 r. 12 kop. (*b*) 40 r. 25 kop. (*c*) 45 r. 20 kop. ?

5.4 Ask for the following items in Russian, without using the genitive case endings:

2 ice creams 4 fruit juices 6 tickets 10 postcards

SHOPPING FOR FOOD

If you want to buy food, go to a **гастроно́м** *gastranom*, a large food store with different departments (or in a smaller place look for **проду́кты** *pradookty* or **продма́г** *pradmag*). Many individual food shops in the Soviet Union simply have signs bearing the name of the product, so for a butcher shop you would see **мя́со** *myasa* (meat), a seafood shop **ры́ба** *ryba* (fish), a bakery **хлеб** *khlep* (bread), a dairy **молоко́** *malako* (milk), and so on. However, you will also see these names of common food shops:

бу́лочная	*boolachnaya*	bakery
конди́терская	*kandityerskaya*	cake shop
моло́чная	*malochnaya*	dairy
о́вощи-фру́кты	*ovashchi-frookty*	produce market
бакале́я	*bakaleya*	grocery store
мя́со-пти́ца	*myasa-ptitsa*	meat and poultry

As well as the produce market, Russians like to buy their fruit and vegetables at the market (**ры́нок** *rynak*), where prices may be high but there is much more variety. Markets are always very busy on weekends and the day before a public holiday, and it's best to go early in the morning. There are sometimes shortages of basic foods in the shops, and fruit and vegetables are generally restricted to what is in season. Though some food shops are now self-service (look for the sign **универса́м** *ooniversam*, supermarket), in many you still have to get in line at the counter and then at the cashier, where you'll need to obtain a receipt (**чек** *chek*) before you can collect your goods.

в гастрономе/in the food store

Alice and Sergei are feeling rather hungry and take a look around a food store. They decide to buy some fruit and some bread.

Sergei: **Ско́лько сто́ят я́блоки?**
Skolka stoyat yablaki?
Assistant: Во́семьдесят копе́ек кило́.
Vosyemdisyat kapeyek kilo.
Sergei: **Я возьму́ кило́**, пожа́луйста, и полкило́ помидо́ров.
Ya vazmoo kilo, pazhalasta, i polkilo pamidoraf.
Alice: Ой, Серге́й, ви́дите како́й краси́вый виногра́д — да́йте нам и виногра́д то́же.
Oi, Sergei, viditye kakoi krasiviy vinagrad — daitye nam i vinagrad tozhe.
(They move on to the bread counter.)
Alice: **Да́йте мне** чёрный хлеб, пожа́луйста, и две* бу́лочки.
Daitye mnye chorniy khlep, pazhalasta, i dvye boolachki.
Assistant: Ещё что́-нибудь?
Yishcho shto-niboot?
Sergei: Да, вон то пиро́жное и эту коро́бку конфе́т.
Da, von to pirozhnaye i etoo karopkoo kanfyet.
Alice: Кака́я жа́дность! У вас по кра́йней ме́ре де́ньги есть?
Kakaya zhadnast! Oo vas po krainyei myeri dyengi yest?
Sergei: Ка́жется у меня́ совсе́м нет ме́лочи . . .
Kazhitsa oo minya savsyem nyet myelachi . . .

ви́дите како́й краси́вый виногра́д	look at those lovely grapes
кака́я жа́дность!	what greed!
по кра́йней ме́ре	at least
Ка́жется у меня́ совсе́м нет ме́лочи . . .	I don't seem to have any change at all . . .

*Remember that you use **две** for "two" with feminine nouns.

Buying something to eat

Don't forget that the metric system of weights and measures operates in the Soviet Union:

Я́блоки сто́ят два рубля́ кило́. *Yablaki stoyat dva rooblya kilo.*	The apples cost 2 rubles a kilo.
Да́йте нам сто грамм/полкило́. *Daitye nam sto gram/polkilo.*	Give us 100 grams, half a kilo.
. . .пятьсо́т грамм помидо́ров/кило́ я́блок *. . .pyatsot gram pamidoraf/kilo yablak*	. . .500 grams of tomatoes/ a kilo of apples

To avoid using the genitive case endings, once again you can simply say:

огурцы́ — пятьсо́т грамм	*agoortsy — pyatsot gram*	cucumbers — 500 g.
пе́рсики — кило́	*persiki — kilo*	peaches — a kilo
я́блоки — два кило́	*yablaki — dva kilo*	apples — 2 kilos

Bread If you go into a **бу́лочная** or a **бу́лочная-конди́терская**, you will find all kinds of different bread and rolls on sale. A **буха́нка** *bookhanka* is a long loaf, usually brown, and a **бато́н** *baton* is a large, round white loaf. Russians are very fond of rye bread (**ржано́й хлеб** *rzhanoi khlep*). You can also buy cake (**кекс** *keks*), candy (**конфе́ты** *konfyety*), and chocolate (**шокола́д** *shakalat*).

Да́йте мне чёрную буха́нку и две бу́лочки. *Daitye mnye chyornuyoo bookhankoo i dvye boolachki.*	Give me a brown loaf and 2 rolls.
. . . вон то пиро́жное и ту коро́бку конфе́т *. . . von to pirozhnaye i too karopkoo kanfyet.*	. . . that pastry and that box of candy.

Use these expressions when buying food:

a bunch of grapes	**кисть виногра́да**	*kist vinograda*
a jar of pickles	**ба́нка солёных**	*banka salyonykh*
a can of sardines	**коро́бка сарди́н**	*karopka sardin*
a box of candy	**коро́бка конфе́т**	*karopka kanfyet*
a bar of chocolate	**пли́тка шокола́да**	*plitka shakalada*

 For a list of groceries, see p.114.

MAKING PURCHASES 2

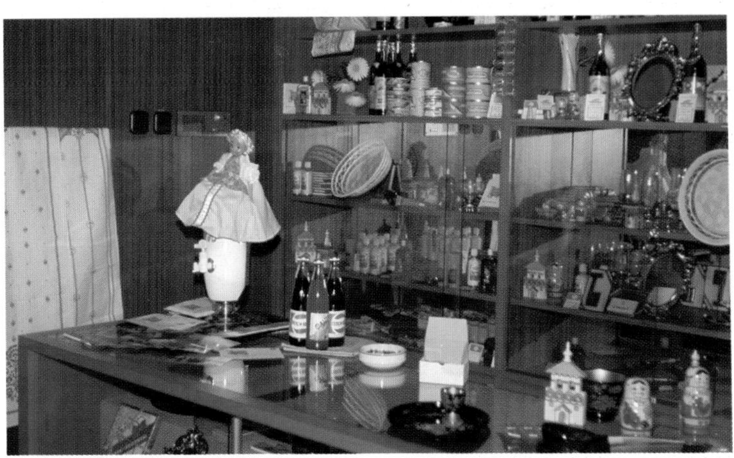

At the **Берёзка** (Beriozka) shops and other hard-currency stores, you can buy souvenirs, food, duty-free liquor, and many other goods for pounds or dollars (though prices may be quoted in rubles). You will also be able to use your credit card (**креди́тная ка́рточка** *kreditnaya kartachka*) for goods bought here and in Intourist hotels. There is often a better choice than you will find outside, but nonetheless you will probably want to look around a typical Russian department store (**универма́г** *oonivermag*), such as **ГУМ** *GUM* — an abbreviation for **Госуда́рственный Универса́льный Магази́н** (State Universal Store) — in Moscow, or **ЦУМ** *TSUM* — **Центра́льный Универса́льный Магази́н** (Central Universal Store) — in Leningrad. Look for these shops or departments: **меха́** *mikha* (furs), **часы́** *chasy* (watches and clocks), **грампласти́нки** *gramplastinki* (records), and **игру́шки** *igrooshki* (toys). Department stores are usually crowded, so be ready to use your elbows, and persevere! Opening times vary from shop to shop, but most are open from 9:00 a.m. to 7:00 or 8:00 p.m. from Monday to Saturday (except on public holidays). Food shops may open earlier and close for lunch between 1:00 and 2:00 p.m. Here are the names of some common shops:

bookshop	**кни́жный магази́н**	*knizhniy magazin*
pharmacy	**апте́ка**	*aptyeka*
electrical goods	**электротова́ры**	*elektratavary*
hardware	**скобяно́й магази́н**	*skabyanoi magazin*
jeweler's	**ювели́рный магази́н**	*yoovilirniy magazin*
music, games, sports, etc.	**культтова́ры**	*kooltavary* (lit. culture goods)
photographic supplies	**фототова́ры**	*fotatavary*
second-hand shop	**комиссио́нный магази́н**	*kamissioniy magazin*
stationery store	**канцтова́ры**	*kantstavary*

The names of many shops begin with **дом** *dom* . . .(which means "house"), e.g., **Дом игру́шки** *Dom igrooshki* (House of the toy), **Дом кни́ги** *Dom knigi* (House of the book), **Дом о́буви** *Dom oboovi* (House of footwear, i.e., shoe store).

Souvenirs When shopping for things to take home, you will find a variety of goods made from amber (**янта́рь** *yantar*), silver (**серебро́** *siribro*), and glass (**стекло́** *stiklo*). Little gifts might include a headscarf (**плато́к** *platok*), shawl (**шаль** *shal*), tablecloth (**ска́терть** *skatirt*), painted wooden spoon (**ло́жка** *lozhka*), or tray (**подно́с** *padnos*). You might also want to buy nested dolls (**матрёшка** *matrioshka*) or a fur cap with earflaps (**уша́нка** *ooshanka*). Here are some more typically Russian items:

abacus	**счёт**	*shchyot*
amber brooch	**янта́рная бро́шка**	*yantarnaya broshka*
amber necklace, earrings	**янта́рные бу́сы, се́рьги**	*yantarnye boosy, sergi*
camera	**фотоаппара́т**	*fotaapparat*
ceramics	**кера́мика**	*keramika*
enamel	**эма́ль**	*emal*
icon	**ико́на**	*ikona*
lace	**кру́жево**	*kroozheva*
leather	**ко́жа**	*kozha*

купить сувениры/buying souvenirs

Alice is looking for presents to take home, and heads for the **Подарки** *Padarki* (Gifts) department in a large store. She has seen a little samovar in the window, and wants to know how much it costs.

Alice:	**Покажи́те,** пожа́луйста, ма́ленький самова́р, кото́рый **в витри́не.** *Pakazhitye, pazhalasta, malinkiy samavar, katory v vitrinye.*
Assistant:	(pointing) Э́тот? *Etat?*
Alice:	**Не э́тот, а тот, ря́дом** — чёрный с цвета́ми. **Да, э́тот! Ско́лько он сто́ит?** *Ni etat, a tot, ryadam — chorny s tsvitami. Da, etat! Skolka on stoit?*
Assistant:	Он сто́ит со́рок пять рубле́й. *On stoit sorak pyat rooblyei.*
Alice:	Бо́же мой, **э́то сли́шком до́рого!** Лу́чше что́-нибудь подеше́вле . . . *Bozhe moi, eta slishkam doraga! Loochshe shto-niboot podishevli . . .*

Бо́же мой! My God!

How to buy something 2

In many shops and stores in the Soviet Union, there are three distinct steps to making purchases:

1 Choosing Ask the salesperson to show you what you want:

Покажи́те пожа́луйста ма́ленький самова́р в витри́не. *Pakazhitye pazhalasta malinkiy samavar v vitrinye.*	Please show me the little samovar in the window.
Не э́тот, а тот, ря́дом. *Ni etat, a tot, ryadam.*	Not this one — that one, next to it.
чёрный с цвета́ми *chorny s tsvitami*	the black one with flowers
Нет, не на́до — это сли́шком до́рого. *Nyet, ni nada — eta slishkam doraga.*	No, I don't want it — it's too expensive.
Лу́чше что́-нибудь подеше́вле. *Loochshe shto-niboot podishevli.*	I'd rather have (lit. better) something cheaper.
Вы́пишите чек, я его́/её возьму́. *Vypishitye chek, ya yevo/yeyo vazmoo.*	Write out a chit, I'll take it.
Плати́те в ка́ссу со́рок пять рубле́й. *Platitye v kassoo sorak pyat rooblyei.*	Pay the cashier, 45 r.

2 Paying Take your chit (**чек** *chek*) and go to the cashier to pay. If you weren't given a chit, you'll need to be able to quote the name of the item, the price (**цена́** *tsena*), and the name or number of the department in the store (e.g., **второ́й отде́л** *vtaroi atdyel*, second department). You'll then get a receipt (another **чек**).

3 Collection Take your receipt back to the first counter, and collect your purchases. In large department stores, you may have to do this at a central collection point (**вы́дача поку́пок** *vydacha pakoopak*). Always keep your final receipt (**това́рный чек** *tavarniy chek*), as you may need to show it at customs when leaving the country.

в универмаге/at the department store

Lucy wants to buy something Russian to wear. She goes into GUM, where she sees some peasant blouses on display in Ladies Wear (**Же́нская Оде́жда** *Zhenskaya Adyezhda*).

Clerk: Что вам ну́жно?
Shto vam noozhna?

Lucy: **Покажи́те, пожа́луйста,** блу́зку.
Pakazhitye, pazhalasta, bloozkoo.

Clerk: Э́ту* кра́сную?
Etoo krasnuyoo?

Lucy: **Нет, не ту*** — бе́лую. **Да, вот э́ту. Мо́жно поме́рить?**
Nyet, ni too — byeluyoo. Da, vot etoo. Mozhna pamyerit?

Clerk: Да, коне́чно. Како́й разме́р?
Da, kanyeshna. Kakoi razmer?

Lucy: Не зна́ю.
Ni znayoo.

Clerk: Ду́маю, э́та блу́зка вам годи́тся.
Doomayoo, eta bloozka vam gaditsa.

(Lucy goes into the changing room and tries the blouse on)

Lucy: **Мне о́чень нра́вится э́та блу́зка. Вы́пишите чек**, пожа́луйста.
Mnye ochin nravitsa eta bloozka. Vypishitye chek, pazhalasta.

Clerk: С удово́льствием. Она́ на вас хорошо́ сиди́т — кака́я вы краси́вая!
S oodavolstviyem. Ana na vas kharasho sidit — kakaya vy krasivaya!

С удово́льствием.	With pleasure.
кака́я вы красивая!	how beautiful you are!

***Э́ту** and **ту** are the accusative forms of **э́та** and **та** — see grammar note.

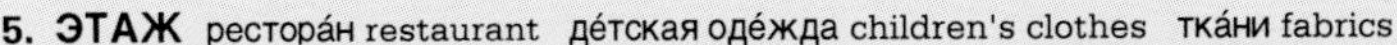

5. ЭТАЖ	рестора́н restaurant де́тская оде́жда children's clothes тка́ни fabrics
4. ЭТАЖ	ме́бель furniture электроприбо́ры electrical goods кафе́ cafe
3. ЭТАЖ	ку́хонная посу́да kitchenware фарфо́р china сувени́ры souvenirs
2. ЭТАЖ	же́нская оде́жда ladies' wear мужска́я оде́жда men's wear о́бувь shoes
1. ЭТАЖ	кни́ги books ка́рты maps духи́ perfumes платки́ scarves зо́нтики umbrellas

Buying clothes

When buying clothes, or anything else for that matter, the easiest thing to do is simply to point to what you want and say **вот э́то** *vot eta* (this one); if the salesperson doesn't get it right at first, you can say **Нет, не э́то, а вот это** *Nyet, ni eta, a vot eta* (No, not this one — *this* one).

Покажи́те, пожа́луйста, бе́лую блу́зку. — Show me the white blouse, please.
Pakazhitye, pazhalasta, byeluyoo bloozkoo.

Не ту — да, вот э́ту. — Not that one — yes, that's it.
Ni too — da, vot etoo.

Мо́жно поме́рить? — Can I try it on?
Mozhna pamyerit?

Како́й разме́р? — What size?
Kakoi razmer?

Мо́жете ли вы снять с меня́ ме́рку? — Can you measure me?
Mozhetye li vy snyat s minya myerkoo?

Ду́маю, что э́та годи́тся. — I think this one will do.
Doomayoo, shto eta gaditsa.

У вас есть то же пла́тье друго́го цве́та? — Do you have this dress in another color?
Oo vas yest to zhe platye droogova tsvyeta?

Оно́ мне велико́/мало́. — It's too big/small for me.
Ano mnye vyeliko/malo.

У вас есть что́-нибудь побо́льше/поме́ньше? — Have you anything bigger/smaller?
Oo vas yest shto-niboot pabolshi/pamyenshi?

Это сли́шком ко́ротко/дли́нно/те́сно. — It's too short/long/tight.
Eta slishkam koratka/dlinna/tyesna.

Ту́фли сли́шком узки́/широки́. *Toofli slishkam oozki/shiraki.*	The shoes are too small/big.
Мне о́чень нра́вится. *Mnye ochin nravitsa.*	I like it very much.
На вас хорошо́ сиди́т. *Na vas kharasho sidit.*	It fits you very well.
Заверни́те, пожа́луйста. *Zavirnitye, pazhalasta.*	Wrap it up, please.
Я про́сто смотрю́. *Ya prosta smatryoo.*	I'm just looking.

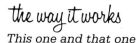

This one and that one

The word for "this" used in a general way is **э́то** *eta*. With a noun it's either:

masc.	*fem.*	*neuter*	*plural*
э́тот по́яс	**э́та** ю́бка	**э́то** пальто́	**э́ти** брю́ки
etat poyas	*eta yoopka*	*eta palto*	*eti bryooki*
this belt	this skirt	this coat	these pants

The word for "that" is **то** *to*:

masc.	*fem.*	*neuter*	*plural*
тот шарф	**та** шу́ба	**то** пла́тье	**те** носки́
tot sharf	*ta shooba*	*to platye*	*tye naski*
that scarf	that fur coat	that dress	those socks

When asking to buy things, for something to eat, etc., you will often find the accusative case is used (e.g., I want *this* blouse, Give me *that* pear):

Я хочу́ **э́ту** блу́зк**у**.	*Ya khachoo etoo bloozkoo.*
Да́йте **ту** гру́ш**у**.	*Daitye too grooshoo.*

If you haven't got any . . .

After a negative statement, such as "I haven't got any . . .," "there isn't any . . .," and so on, you will find the genitive case used in Russian. There are quite a few examples of this in the dialogues to date. Here are some more:

У нас **нет** хле́б**а**/молок**а́**/яи́ц. *Oo nas nyet khlyeba/malaka/yaits.*	We don't have any bread/milk/eggs.
У вас есть де́ньги? — У меня́ **нет** де́нег.* *Oo vas yest dyengi? — Oo minya nyet dyenek.*	Do you have any money? — I have no money.
У вас есть ме́лочь? — У меня́ **нет** ме́лоч**и**. *Oo vas yest myelach? — Oo minya nyet myelachi.*	Do you have any change? — I don't have any change.

***де́нег** is the genitive plural of **де́ньги** (money) and you will probably hear both words quite frequently!

I like it, I don't like it

If you are talking about liking something specific, rather than in a general way, then use the expression **мне нра́вится** *mnye nravitsa* (lit. it is pleasing to me):

Э́та руба́шка мне о́чень нра́вится, . . . *Eta roobashka mnye ochin nravitsa...*	I like this shirt very much . . .
. . . а сви́тер мне совсе́м не нра́вится *. . . a sviter mnye savsyem ni nravitsa*	. . . but I don't like the sweater at all

For words in the plural, use **мне нра́вятся** *mnye nravyatsa*.

things to do

.5 You are buying food for a picnic and jot down a few of the things you need. How much money must you spend in order to buy these items: **пятьсо́т грамм помидо́ров, два кило́ я́блок, кило́ груш, пли́тка шокола́да?**

.6 **В бу́лочной** You are feeling rather hungry and are tempted by the smells coming from a bakery. See if you can ask for what you want.

Assistant:	Что вам ну́жно?
You:	(You want a round loaf.)
Assistant:	Ещё что́-нибудь?
You:	(You'd like two bread rolls and a pastry.)

.7 You go into a department store determined to buy something to wear. Can you talk to the assistant?

Продавщи́ца:	Вы что́-нибудь хоти́те?
Вы:	(Ask her to show you the green shirt in the window.)
Продавщи́ца:	Э́ту?
Вы:	(No, not that one, the one next to it . . . Ask her the price.)
Продавщи́ца:	Сто́ит два́дцать пять рубле́й.
Вы:	(You won't take it, it's too expensive.)

5.8 You want to buy the items on the left, but which shops should you go to? Match up the goods with the shops on the right.

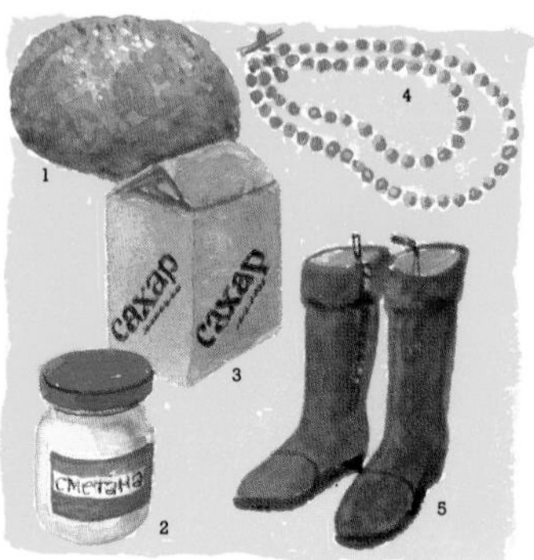

(*a*) бакале́я
(*b*) дом о́буви
(*c*) бу́лочная
(*d*) моло́чная
(*e*) ювели́рный магази́н

5.9 Ско́лько они́ сто́ят? You point to various things you want to buy in a department store, and the assistant tells you the prices — but you're not sure you've heard correctly, so you ask her **Напиши́те, пожа́луйста** (Please write it down). Can you match what she said (on the left) to what she writes (on the right)?

1 Сто́ит рубль пятьдеся́т копе́ек
2 Сто́ят шестьдеся́т копе́ек.
3 Сто́ит пять рубле́й.
4 Сто́ит во́семь рубле́й со́рок копе́ек.

книга 5р
пластинка 1р.50к
открытки 60к
счёт 8р.40к

5.10 You have finally chosen these articles in the souvenir department as gifts to take home, and the assistant tells you to pay the cashier. Can you tell the cashier (*a*) the name of the department (*b*) the name of each item (*c*) the price?

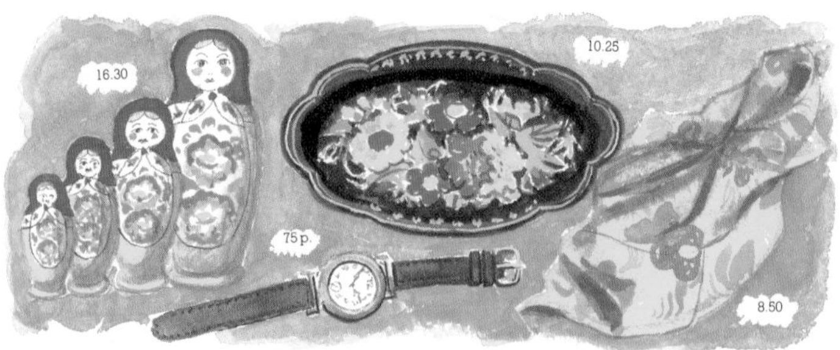

MEDICAL PROBLEMS

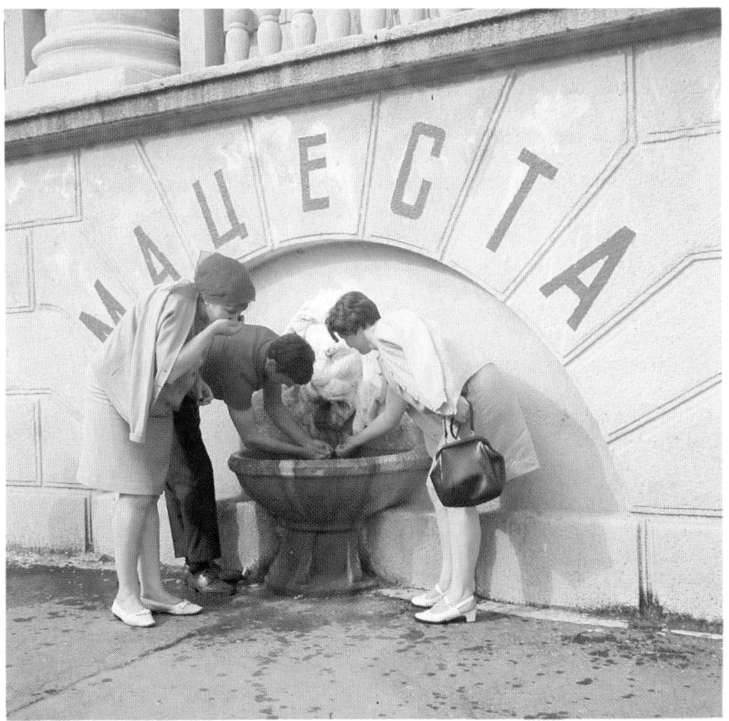

If you become ill in the Soviet Union, ask your hotel or Intourist Bureau to call the duty doctor. Medical treatment is free, though some medicines may not be. Hospital treatment will have to be paid for on the spot, so it's advisable to take out adequate medical insurance. Many Western medicines simply cannot be found, so if you rely on certain pills or medicines, don't forget to bring them with you. In Moscow, the special clinic for foreigners is at Gruzinsky Pereulok 3, Korpus 2.

The Russian health service runs on a system of polyclinics, and there are no GPs. However, Russians like to use herbal and simple home remedies for minor illnesses. Spas and health cure vacations combining sea or mountain air, mineral waters, physiotherapy, etc., are extremely popular, and Intourist can arrange for tourists to take treatment at resort towns in the Caucasus or Crimea. Go to the pharmacy for basic medicines such as aspirin (look for the sign **Дежу́рная Апте́ка** *Dizhoornaya Aptyeka*, pharmacy on night duty), but do not expect to find an enormous range of toiletries — it's advisable to take such things as tampons and cosmetics with you.

у меня простуда/I've got a cold

Mike Nash and his group have arrived in Yalta, where they are to spend the next two days relaxing on the Black Sea coast. Lena was hoping to organize an excursion in the afternoon, but unfortunately Mike isn't feeling too good . . .

Lena: Что с ва́ми, Майк? Вам пло́хо?
Shto s vami, Mike? Vam plokha?

Mike: Да, **я о́чень не хорошо́ себя́ чу́вствую. У меня́ боли́т** го́рло — и голова́. Ду́маю, что мне ну́жен врач.
Da, ya ochin ni kharasho sibya choostvuyoo. Oo minya balit gorla — i galava. Doomayoo, shto mnye noozhen vrach.

Lena: У вас есть температу́ра? Э́то вероя́тно просту́да, и́ли грипп. Пойдём сперва́ в апте́ку.
Oo vas yest timperatoora? Eta virayatna prastooda, ili greepp. Paeedyom spirva v aptyekoo.

Вам пло́хо? Aren't you well?
вероя́тно probably
У меня́ боли́т го́рло — и голова́ I've got a headache — and a sore throat
врач doctor
сперва́ first of all

в аптеке/at the pharmacy

Mike: **У вас есть что́-нибудь от** гри́ппа?
Oo vas yest shto-niboot at greeppa?

Pharmacist: Дава́йте посмо́трим . . . Вот — принима́йте э́ти табле́тки три ра́за в день, по́сле еды́.
Davaitye pasmotrim . . . Vot — prinimaitye eti tabletki tree raza v dyen, posli yedy.

Mike: Спаси́бо. **Мо́жете дать мне та́кже** табле́тки для го́рла?
Spaseeba. Mozhetye dat mnye takzhe tablyetki dlya gorla?

Pharmacist: К сожале́нию у меня́ нет таки́х табле́ток . . . я порекоменду́ю но́вое полоска́ние для го́рла. У него́ о́чень прия́тный вкус!
K sazhalyeniyoo oo minya nyet takikh tablyetak . . . ya parikamyenduyoo novaye palaskaniye dlya gorla. Oo nyevo ochin priyatniy vkoos!

что́-нибудь для гриппа something for the flu
три ра́за 3 times
полоска́ние gargle
У него́ о́чень прия́тный вкус! It tastes very nice!

I don't feel very well

Что с вами . . . вам пло́хо?
Shto s vami . . .vam plokha?
What's the matter . . . aren't you feeling well?

Я пло́хо/нехорошо́ чу́вствую себя́.
Ya plokha/nikharasho choostvuyoo sibya.
I feel ill.

Что у вас боли́т?
Shto oo vas baleet?
Where does it hurt?

У меня́ боли́т голова́/ го́рло/па́лец/зуб.
Oo minya baleet galava/gorla/palyets/zoop.
I've got a headache/sore throat/finger/tooth.

У меня́ просту́да/температу́ра/грипп.
Oo minya prastooda/timperatoora/greepp.
I've got a cold/ temperature/flu.

У меня́ запо́р/поно́с/несваре́ние желу́дка.
Oo minya zapor/panos/nisvaryeniye zhelootka.
I've got constipation/ diarrhea/indigestion.

Меня́ тошни́т/меня́ рвёт.
Minya tashnit/minya rvyot.
I feel nauseous/I've been vomiting.

У меня́ со́лнечный уда́р/уку́с насеко́мого.
Oo minya solnichniy oodar/ookoos nasikomava.
I have sunstroke/ an insect bite.

Я поре́зал * но́гу/обжёг ру́ку.
Ya paryezal nogoo/abzhog rookoo.
I've cut my foot/burned my hand.

У меня́ синя́к/поре́з/растяже́ние свя́зок.
Oo minya sinyak/paryez/rastyazheniye svyazak.
I have a buise/cut/sprain.

Я слома́л/слома́ла себе́ . . .
Ya slamal/slamala sibye . . .
I have broken . . .

Мне ну́жен врач.
Mnye noozhen vrach.
I need a doctor.

*If it's a woman talking, you add **а** to the past tense endings: я поре́зала . . . (see grammar section on p. 93 for more about the past tense).

See p. 115 for a list of parts of the body.

Things the doctor should know

Я астма́тик/диабе́тик.
Ya astmatik/diabetik.
I'm asthmatic/diabetic.

У меня сенна́я лихора́дка/больно́е се́рдце.
Oo minya sinnaya likharadka/balnoye sertse.
I have hay fever/ heart trouble.

Я не переношу́ пеницилли́н/антибио́тики.
Ya ni pirinashoo pyenitsilin/antibiotiki.
I can't take penicillin/ antibiotics.

Я принима́ю э́ти пилю́ли/табле́тки.
Ya prinimayoo eti pilyooli/tablyetki.
I'm taking these pills/ tablets.

Я бере́менна.
Ya biryeminna.
I'm pregnant.

Я принима́ю противозача́точные таблетки.
Ya prinimayoo prativazachatachnye tablyetki.
I'm on the pill.

At the pharmacy

У вас есть что́-нибудь от гри́ппа/просту́ды/ тошноты́?
Oo vas yest shto-niboot at greeppa/prastoody/ tashnaty?
Have you got something for flu/cold/nausea?

Принима́йте э́то лека́рство/э́ти табле́тки.
Prinimaitye eta likarstva/eti tablyetki.
Take this medicine/these tablets.

ка́ждые четы́ре часа́/три ра́за в день
kazhdye chitirye chasa/tree raza v dyen
every four hours/three times a day

по ча́йной ло́жке/по́сле еды́, пе́ред едо́й
po chainoi lozhki/posli yedy, peryed yedoi
one teaspoonful/after meals, before meals

Вам ну́жен врач.
Vam noozhen vrach.
You need a doctor.

Here are some things you might want to buy at the pharmacy:

aspirin	**аспири́н** *aspirin*
bandage	**бинт** *bint*
contraceptives	**противозача́точные сре́дства** *prativazachatachniye sredstva*
cotton	**ва́та** *vata*
gargle	**полоска́ние** *palaskaniye dlya gorla*
ointment	**мазь** *maz*
adhesive tape	**пла́стырь** *plastyr*
insect repellent	**сре́дство от камаро́в** *sredstva at kamarof*
laxative	**слаби́тельное** *slabitelnaye*
throat lozenges	**табле́тки для го́рла** *tablyetki dlya gorla*
sanitary napkins	**гигиени́ческие салфе́тки** *gigienicheskiye salfyetki*

АПТЕКА

For a list of toiletries, see p. 115.

GETTING A SNACK/TALKING ABOUT THE WEATHER

в закусочной/at the snack bar

On the way back from the pharmacy, Lena begins to feel the pangs of hunger. Although it's very hot and Mike still isn't well, she persuades him to stop at a snack bar.

Lena: Что вам уго́дно? Есть бутербро́ды с колбасо́й, с икро́й и́ли с сы́ром. У них та́кже пирожки́ с ри́сом, с капу́стой и́ли с мя́сом.
Shto vam oogodna? Yest booterbrody s kalbasoi, s ikroi ili s syram. Oo nikh takzhe pirazhki s risam, s kapoostoi ili s myasyam.

Mike: **Я совсе́м не го́лоден,** но **мне о́чень хо́чется пить.** Сего́дня **так жа́рко.**
Ya savsyem ni galodyen, no mnye ochin khochitsa peet. Sivodnya tak zharko.

Lena: Да, **хоро́шая пого́да.** Здесь всегда́ сия́ет со́лнце, да́же зимо́й. Мно́го люде́й отдыха́ют в Я́лте! Но скажи́те, Майк, вы хорошо́ говори́те по-ру́сски — вы родили́сь в Великобрита́нии, пра́вда?
Da, kharoshaya pagoda. Zdyes vsikda siyaet sonsti, dazhe zimoi. Mngo lyoodyei atdykhayoot v Yalti! No skazhitye, Mike, vy kharasho gavaritye pa-roosski — vy radilis v Vyelikobritanii, pravda?

Mike: Да, но у меня́ ру́сская ба́бушка — а жена́ америка́нка, из Вашингто́на.
Da, no oo minya roosskaya babooshka — a zhena amerikanka, iz Vashingtona.

Lena: Интере́сно!.. Вот на́ши напи́тки. Дава́йте вы́пьем за междунаро́дную дру́жбу!
Intiryesna! . . . Vot nashi napitki. Davaitye vypyem za myezhdoonarodnuyoo droozhboo!

Я не го́лоден.	I'm not hungry.
Так жа́рко.	It's so hot.
ба́бушка, жена	grandmother, wife
мне хо́чется пить	I feel like drinking
со́лнце	the sun
Мно́го люде́й отдыха́ют в Я́лте.	Lots of people vacation at Yalta.
Вы родили́сь . . . , пра́вда?	You were born . . . , weren't you?
Дава́йте вы́пьем за междунаро́дную дру́жбу!	Let's drink to international friendship!

If you're feeling hungry between meals, or you want a snack for lunch, here are some of the things you might find at a cafe or snack bar:

бутербро́д с колбасо́й/ с икро́й	*booterbrod s kalbasoi/ikroi*	a salami/caviar sandwich
пирожки́	*pirazhki*	patties, stuffed dumplings
сарде́льки	*sardyelki*	little sausages, frankfurters
копчёная колбаса́	*kapchonaya kalbasa*	smoked sausage
пиро́г с мя́сом	*pirog s myasam*	meat pie
пиро́г с ри́сом/с капу́стой	*pirog s risam/ s kapoostoi*	rice/cabbage pie
жа́реная карто́шка	*zharinaya kartoshka*	french fries
сы́рники, ола́дьи	*syrniki, oladi*	cheese cakes, thick pancakes

Weather If you visit the Soviet Union between November and March, don't forget that it can be extremely cold. For outdoor wear you'll need a thick overcoat, warm gloves, and most important, a hat that covers your ears. Hotel rooms are usually well heated. In the South it may be warm from April onwards, and wherever you go you can expect a fair amount of hot, sunny weather from May to the end of August — but take your umbrellas, as there will almost certainly be the occasional summer shower.

Какáя сегóдня погóда? *What's the weather like today?*

Хорóшая погóда/Плохáя погóда. *Kharoshaya pagoda/Plokhaya pagoda.* — It's fine/It's bad weather.

Жáрко/Хóлодно. *Zharka/Kholadna.* — It's hot/It's cold.

Тепló/Вéтрено. *Tiplo/Vetrino.* — It's warm/It's windy.

Сегóдня тумáн. *Sivodnya tooman.* — It's foggy today.

Идёт дождь/снег. *Idyot dozhd/snyek.* — It's raining/snowing.

Морóзит. *Marozit.* — It's freezing.

Сóлнце всегдá сиúет, дáже зимóй. *Sontsi vsikda siyaet, dazhe zimoi.* — The sun always shines, even in winter.

Languages and nationalities

Вы óчень хорошó говорúте по-рýсски/по-английски. *Vy ochin kharasho gavaritye pa-roossky/pa-anglisky.* — You speak Russian/English very well.

Вы родилúсь в Великобритáнии/США? *Vy radilis v Vyelikobritanii/Se-She-Ah?* — Were you born in Great Britain/USA?

Я англичáнин/англичáнка/америкáнец/америкáнка. *Ya anglichanin/anglichanka/amerikanits/amerikanka.* — I'm English/American.

the way it works

У меня болúт . . .

This expression means "My . . . hurts." If you want to say his or her or their . . . hurts, you use **у него** *oo nyevo,* **у неё** *oo nyeyo* or **у них** *oo nikh:*

У негó болúт ногá. *Oo nyevo balit naga.* His leg hurts/He has a sore leg.

"Our" and "their"

The word for "our" is **наш** (*nash*). It works like **ваш: на́ши напи́тки** *nashi napitki* (our drinks). If you want to say "their," use **их: их заку́ски** *ikh zakooski* (their snacks).

Пиро́г с триба́ми *Pie with mushrooms*
(The instrumental case)

There are many uses for the instrumental case, the main one being to denote the instrument by means of which you do something, e.g.:

Я пишу́ ру́ч**кой** *Ya pishoo roochkoi* I write with a pen. (**ру́чка** = pen)

This case is always used after **с** *s* (with). You have already seen all of these:

masc. (and neuter)	*feminine*	*plural*
с мя́с**ом** *s myasam*	с икр**о́й** *s ikroi*	с гриб**а́ми** *s gribami*

Other nouns take similar endings in the instrumental. Note that **с** is often used when we would say "and," e.g., **мя́со с карто́шкой** (meat and potatoes), **хлеб с ма́слом** (bread and butter).

Pronouns in the instrumental are as follows: **мной, тобо́й, им, ей, на́ми, ва́ми, и́ми**. After prepositions, they are

со* мной	*sa mnoi*	with me	**с на́ми**	*s nami*	with us
с тобо́й	*s taboi*	with you	**с ва́ми**	*s vami*	with you
с ним	*s neem*	with him/it	**с ни́ми**	*s nimi*	with them
с ней	*s nyei*	with her/it			

*In some expressions **с** adds an **о**

Here is another use of **с**:

мы с ва́ми *my s vami* you and I **мы с Майком** *my s Mikam* Mike and I

The instrumental is also used after the prepositions **пе́ред** *pyerid* (before), **за** *za* (behind), and **над** *nad* (above, over).

things to do

1 You become ill on the beach, and the doctor doesn't seem to understand much English. Can you describe your symptoms?

Врач: Расскажи́те, что у вас боли́т?
Вы: (You've got a stomachache.)
Врач: Что ещё?
Вы: (Yes, a headache and you feel sick.)
Врач: У вас высо́кая температу́ра — это вероя́тно со́лнечный уда́р.

Did you understand the diagnosis?

6.2 Various guests at your hotel are suffering from a number of ailments. Can you explain to the doctor what is the matter with each of them?

1. Joanna: she's got a sore foot.
2. Peter: he's got a bad back.
3. Cathy: indigestion.
4. Simon: an insect bite.
5. Julia: a cold.

6.3 Now you've been sent to the pharmacy to buy supplies for members of your group.

1 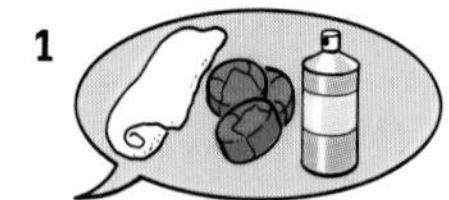 cotton, throat lozenges, and insect repellent

2  some toothpaste, soap, and razor blades

3  something for diarrhea

6.4 All that sea air has made you feel hungry, so you and a friend go into a cafe for a snack. Ask for the following:

cheese sandwich

a caviar sandwich 

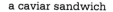

a meat pie

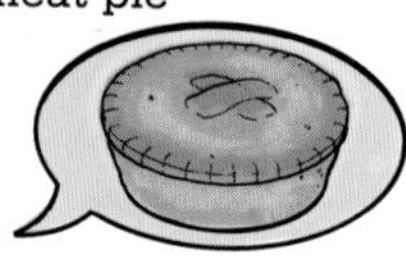

some cheese cakes

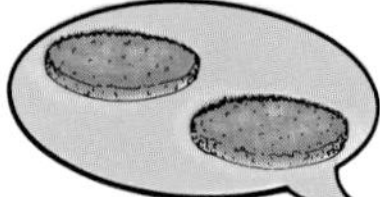

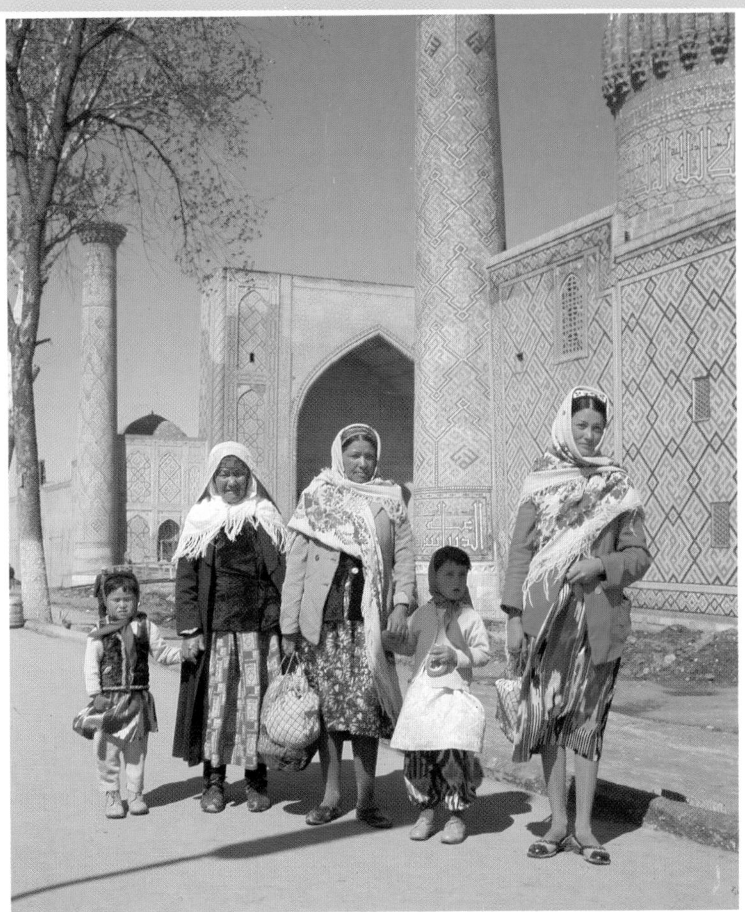

Asian USSR It is hard to believe that the Central Asian Soviet republics are part of the same country as the western republics. The people here have different features, wear different dress, and speak different languages. The official language is Russian, however, and you will find names of streets, shops, buildings, etc., in Russian as well as the same type of municipal buildings and statues of Lenin that can be found all over the country, from Moscow to Vladivostok. With the Russian you have learned, you will be able to make yourself understood wherever you go in the Soviet Union!

Tashkent, the capital of Uzbekistan, contains large modern hotels and modern apartment buildings, yet the Eastern customs prevail. In the museums you will see oriental pottery and jewelry, splendid rugs and silks, and the distinctive colorful embroidery and embroidered skullcaps of the region.

STAMPS AND POST OFFICES

марки купить/buying stamps

After a lightning tour of the city on a wet morning, Lucy has bought some postcards with views of Tashkent. She goes to the hotel shop for some stamps.

Lucy: **Ско́лько сто́ит откры́тка в А́нглию,** пожа́луйста?
Skolka stoit atkrytka v Angliyoo, pazhalasta?

Assistant: В А́нглию? Три́дцать пять копе́ек.
V Angliyoo? Tritsat pyat kapeyek.

Lucy: **Две ма́рки,** пожа́луйста, и **одну́ для письма́ в Кана́ду.**
Dvye marki, pazhalasta, i adnoo dlya pisma v Kanadoo.

Assistant: Авиаписьмо́? Вот. Оно́ сто́ит . . . (She adds up the amount. Lucy pays and turns to go) Де́вушка, не забу́дьте зо́нтик!
Aviapismo? Vot. Ano stoit . . . Dyevooshka, ni zaboodtye zontik!

две ма́рки two stamps
письмо́ a letter
Не забу́дьте зо́нтик. Don't forget your umbrella.

Lucy bought her stamps at the hotel shop, where they also sell postcards, writing paper (**почто́вая бума́га** *pachtovaya boomaga*), and envelopes (**конве́рты** *kanvyerty*). However, she might equally well have gone to the post office.

Post offices offer postal, telegram, telephone, and telex facilities, and are open from 9:00 a.m. to 6:00 or 7:00 p.m. As well as buying stamps, etc., you can send international telegrams (look for the sign **Междунаро́дная Телегра́мма**, and pick up a form — **междунаро́дный бланк** *mizhdoonarodniy blank*). If you want to send a parcel home, hand over the *contents* to the counter clerk and ask him or her to wrap them (**заверни́те** *zavirnitye*). Then your parcel will be weighed and stamped, you'll be asked to write your address on the back, and given a receipt.

Many large hotels contain a branch of the post office on the premises, and most transactions can be conducted here fairly easily!

На по́чте *At the post office*

Где я могу́ купи́ть ма́рки? *Gdye ya magoo koopit marki?*	Where can I buy stamps?
Вон там, в окне́ пять. *Von tam, v aknye pyat.*	Over there, at counter 5.
Ско́лько сто́ит откры́тка в А́нглию? *Skolka stoit atkrytka v Angliyoo?*	How much is a postcard to England?
Ско́лько сто́ит письмо́ в Кана́ду? *Skolka stoit pismo v Kanadoo?*	How much is a letter to Canada?
а́виаписьмо/посы́лка/перево́д *aviapismo/pasylka/pirivod*	an airmail letter/a parcel/money order
ма́рка за пятьдеся́т копе́ек *marka za pitdisyat kapeyek*	a 50-kopeck stamp
две ма́рки/пять ма́рок за . . . копе́ек *dvye marki/pyat marak za . . . kapeyek*	two/five stamps at . . . kopecks
Я хочу́ посла́ть заказно́е письмо́. *Ya khachoo paslat zakaznoye pismo.*	I want to send a registered letter.
Где по́чта до востре́бования? *Gdye pochta da vastrebavaniya?*	Where is the general delivery counter?
Где почто́вый я́щик? *Gdye pachtovy yashchik?*	Where's the mailbox?

MAKING A PHONE CALL

разговор по телефону/telephone conversation

Meanwhile, there is something of a crisis in the hotel lobby, as Donald has discovered his wallet is missing. He thinks he may have left it in the teahouse they visited in the morning, so Vadim makes a quick phone call on his behalf. Having ascertained the number, he picks up the receiver and dials.

Vadim: Нет, не отвеча́ют . . . а, вот кто́-то!
Nyet, ni atvyechayoot . . . a, vot kto-ta!

Manager: Алло́, слу́шаю.
Allo, slooshayoo.

Vadim: **Алло́, э́то говори́т** Вади́м И́горевич Григо́рьев. Извини́те, но ка́жется мы сего́дня у́тром оста́вили у вас бума́жник.
Allo, eta gavarit Vadim Igorevich Grigorev. Izvinitye, no kazhitsa my sivodnya ootram astavili oo vas boomazhnik.

Manager: Подожди́те одну́ мину́точку . . . (returning) Алло́? Мо́жете описа́ть бума́жник? Како́го цве́та, наприме́р?
Padazhditye adnoo minootachkoo . . . Allo? Mozhetye apisat boomazhnik? Kakova tsvyeta, naprimer?

Vadim: Э́то о́чень большо́й бума́жник, из кори́чневой ко́жи.
Eta ochen balshoi boomazhnik, iz karichnyevoi kozhi.

Manager: О́чень жаль. Кто́-то оста́вил у нас кра́сную су́мочку, а бума́жников нет.
Ochin zhal. Kto-ta astavil oo nas krasnuyoo soomachkoo, a boomazhnikof nyet.

Ка́жется мы оста́вили у вас бума́жник.	It seems we left a wallet at your place.
описа́ть	describe
наприме́р	for example
из кори́чневой ко́жи	in brown leather
кто́-то	someone

Using the telephone It's very cheap to make local phone calls in the Soviet Union. In large cities there are plenty of public phone booths (**телефо́н автома́т** *tilifon aftamat*) and the procedure is simple. Lift the receiver, insert 2 kopecks, wait for the dial tone and dial the number (**но́мер** *nomir*).

To phone intercity or abroad you should either go to a post office (the sign to look for is **Междунаро́дный телефо́нный перегово́рный пункт**, international telephone call point) where you'll be directed to a cabin (**каби́на** *kabina*) when your call eventually comes through, or make the call through your hotel.

По телефо́ну *On the phone*

Мне ну́жно позвони́ть в А́нглию/США. *Mnye noozhna pazvanit v Angliyoo/Se-She-Ah.*	I need to phone England/ the USA.
Мо́жно позвони́ть? Мне ну́жен э́тот но́мер. *Mozhna pazvanit? Mnye noozhyen etat nomir.*	Can I make a phone call? I need this number.
Я хочу́ звони́ть Вади́му/Ле́не. *Ya khachoo zvanit Vadimoo/Lenye.*	I want to phone Vadim/ Lena.
Его́/её нет до́ма. *Yevo/yeyo nyet doma.*	He/she is not at home.
За́нято/Э́то оши́бка. *Zanyata/Eta ashipka.*	It's busy/It's the wrong number.
Не отвеча́ют. *Ni atvyechayoot.*	There's no reply.
Вас про́сят к телефо́ну. *Vas prosyat k tilifonoo.*	You're wanted on the phone.
Алло́, слу́шаю. *Allo, slooshayoo.*	Hello, (I'm listening).
Кто говори́т? Это Вади́м говори́т. *Kto gavarit? Eta Vadim gavarit.*	Who's speaking? This is Vadim.
Подожди́те одну́ мину́точку. *Padazhditye adnoo minootachkoo.*	Hold the line a minute.

EMERGENCIES

With any luck, your visit to the Soviet Union will be trouble free, and any minor problems will be sorted out by your guide or Intourist Bureau. If you are out and about on your own and you or a companion is involved in an accident, there is an emergency ambulance service to call. If you have a car accident you should register it at once with the traffic police and obtain a written form for insurance purposes. Here are some expressions we hope you won't need to use.

В слу́чае кра́йней необходи́мости *In case of emergency*

На по́мощь! *Na pomashch!*	Help!
Где ближа́йшее отделе́ние мили́ции? *Gdye blizhaisheye atdilyeniye militsii?*	Where's the nearest police station?
Я потеря́л/потеря́ла бума́жник *Ya patiryal/patiryala boomazhnik*	I have lost my wallet
часы́/су́мочку/биле́ты/кошелёк. *chasy/soomachkoo/bilyety/kashelyok.*	my watch/handbag/tickets/ purse.
Я заблуди́лся/заблуди́лась. *Ya zabloodilsa/zabloodilas.*	I'm lost.
Позвони́те в мили́цию/врачу́. *Pazvanitye v militsiyoo/vrachoo.*	Call the police/a doctor.

пожáрная охрáна *pazharnaya akhrana*	the fire department
скóрая пóмощь *skoraya pomashch*	first aid (ambulance)
Держи́ вóра! *Dirzhi vora!*	Stop thief!
Бритáнское посóльство *Britanskaye pasolstva*	British Embassy
Ýлица Чайкóвского 19/21/23 *Oolitsa Chaikovskava 19/21/23*	Tchaikovsky Street 19/21/23 (address of the U.S. Embassy in Moscow)

the way it works

-то, -нибудь

These endings can be added to mean "some . . ." (**-то** is more specific, **-нибудь** is undiscriminating and has the sense "someone/thing, etc., or other"):

ктó-то	*kto-ta*	someone
чтó-нибудь	*shto-niboot*	something
гдé-то	*gdye-ta*	somewhere

Я должнá позвони́ть Ивáну *I must phone Ivan*
(The dative case)

This case is used when we would often say "to," e.g.:

Я пишý Михайлу *Ya pishoo Mikhailoo* I am writing to Mikhail

Sometimes the "to" is omitted in English:

Я звоню́ Вéр**е**. *Ya zvanyoo Verye.*	I am phoning (lit. "to") Vera.
Я пишý Михайл**у** письмó. *Ya pishoo Mikhailoo pismo.*	I am writing Mikhail a letter.

In this last sentence, the letter is the *direct object* and Mikhail is the *indirect object*. Many nouns in the dative case behave as follows:

masc.	*neuter*	*fem.*	*plural*
телефóн**у**	мéст**у**	пóчт**е**	бумáжник**ам**
tilifonoo	*myestoo*	*pochtye*	*boomazhnikam*

Masculine nouns ending in a soft sign and neuter nouns ending in **-е** take **-ю**: **пóлю**. Feminine nouns ending in a soft sign take **-и** and those ending in **-ия** change to **-ии: нóчи, стáнции**. Feminine nouns ending in **-я** change to **-е**: **Тóне.**

You will also find the dative used after these verbs:

расскáзывать *raskazyvat* (to tell), **объясня́ть** *abyisnyat* (to explain), **приноси́ть** *prinasit* (to bring).

Adjectives in the dative end in **ому/ему** for masculine, **ой/ей** for feminine.

You already know some of the pronouns in the dative case. Here is the full list:

мне *mnye* (to) me	**нам** *nam* (to) us
тебé *tibye* (to) you	**вам** *vam* (to) you
емý *yemoo* (**нему** after a prep.) (to) him	**им** *im* (**ним** after a prep.) (to) them
ей *yei* (**ней** after a prep.) (to) her	

The dative case is used after the prepositions **по** *po* (along, by) and **к** *k* (to, toward).

Кáжется

This means literally "it seems," and you will hear it used quite a lot in Russian, often with the sense of "apparently": **Кáжется вáжное лицó** *Kazhitsa vazhnaye litso*: Apparently it's an important person. **Кáжется** is often used with **мне, вас,** etc.:

Мне кáжется, что . . .	*Mnye kazhitsa, shto . . .*	It seems to me that . . .

There are many other so-called impersonal expressions in Russian. Here are some more:

Мне хóлодно. *Mnye kholadna.*	I'm cold (lit. It is cold to me).
Нам скýчно. *Nam skooshna.*	We're bored (lit. It's boring to us).
Вам хóчется обрáтно? *Vam khochitsa abratna?*	Do you feel like going back?

An introduction to the past tense

You will have noticed the past tense endings in many of the phrases to date. To form the past tense, you simply remove the infinitive ending from a verb and substitute **л** *l* (masculine), **ло** *lo* (neuter), **ла** *la* (feminine), or **ли** *li* (plural):

Дóналд потеря**л** бумáжник. *Donald patiryal boomazhnik.*	Donald lost his wallet.
Тóня остáви**ла** сýмочку в чайхáне. *Tonya astavila soomachkoo v chaikhani.*	Tonya left her bag in the teahouse.
Они́ звони́**ли** хозя́ину. *Ani zvanili khazyainoo.*	They phoned the manager.

Some verbs have irregular past tense endings, e.g.:

идти́	(to go)	**шёл**	*shol*	**шло**	*shlo*	**шла**	*shla*	**шли**	*shli*
мочь	(to be able)	**мог**	*mok*	**моглó**	*muglo*	**моглá**	*mugla*	**могли́**	*mugli*

You will probably hear the verb "to be" (**быть** *byt*) used in the past tense:

он был	*on byl*	he was	**онó бы́ло**	*ano byla*	it was
онá былá	*ana byla*	she was	**они́ бы́ли**	*ani byli*	they were

things to do

5 You have various things to send home, so you go into a post office. Can you communicate in Russian?

1. You want to send a letter to the United States. Ask how much it is.
2. You want two stamps at 50 kopecks.
3. Tell the clerk you want to send an international telegram and ask for the form.
4. You want to have a parcel wrapped and to know how much it costs. What do you say?

6 Problems with the phone . . .

1. You are sitting in your hotel lounge when an employee comes up to you and says: **Вас про́сят к телефо́ну.** What's going on?
2. You rush to the phone, and this is what you hear: **Алло́, э́то Мари́на Петро́вна?** Assuming this isn't the case, what do you reply?
3. You decide to make a phone call home, and eventually you get through to the operator, who says: **Подожди́те одну́ мину́ту.** What is she telling you?

7 Here are some examples of the things that Lucy's group has inadvertently mislaid. Can you say what each of them is in Russian? Begin: **Мы потеря́ли . . .**

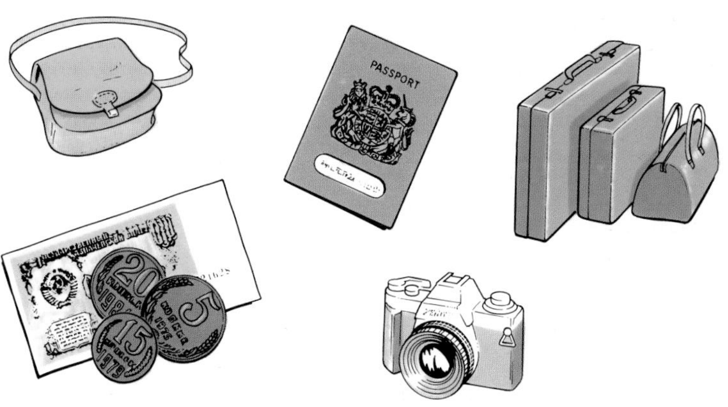

SPORTS AND LEISURE

Leisure activities There are plenty of opportunities to practice sports in the Soviet Union, as main cities have large modern sports centers, such as the Kirov Stadium in Leningrad or the Luzhniki Sports Center in Moscow, with its skating rinks and tennis courts. You will find swimming pools everywhere, particularly open-air heated pools, which are open summer and winter alike, and taking saunas is somewhat of a national pastime. You can rent skis, sleds, and skates for use in the Moscow and Leningrad parks and there is cross-country skiing around Moscow, but for more serious mountain skiing, you should join a trip to the Caucasus. Intourist also arranges hunting trips to the Caucasus mountains, Siberia, and the Ukraine, with all equipment provided. Ice hockey (**хокке́й** *khakhei*) and soccer (**футбо́л** *footbol*) are among the most popular games in the Soviet Union, and athletics (**атле́тика** *atlyetika*) have a large following. Tickets for soccer games can be bought from the stadium or, in Moscow, from Metro station stands.

Camping If you want to camp, you'll need to take a car. Camping is still very primitive and you won't find any luxury facilities. You will have to make arrangements in advance and pay with Intourist camping vouchers (**тало́ны** *talony*). You can rent a tent, and at most campsites (**ке́мпинги** *kempingi*) ready-cooked meals are available. Many sites are only open for three months in the summer.

у моря/by the sea

Mike and Alice are up early on Sunday morning. It is a lovely day, the water looks inviting, and Mike is trying to persuade Lena to come for a swim.

Mike: Смотри́те, сего́дня мо́ре тако́е споко́йное. **Пойдём купа́ться**! Ле́на, у вас есть купа́льный костю́м?
Smatritye, sivodnya morye takoye spakoinaye. Paeedyom koopatsa! Lyena, oo vas yest koopalniy kastyoom?

Lena: Я пло́хо пла́ваю, **но о́чень люблю́ игра́ть в** те́ннис. Вы лю́бите спорт? Здесь прекра́сные те́ннисные ко́рты ря́дом с гости́ницей — и́ли **мо́жно взять** ло́дки **напрока́т**.
Ya plokha plavayoo, no ochin lyooblyoo igrat v tenis. Vy lyoobitye sport? Zdyes prikrasnye tennisnye korty ryadam s gastinitsei — ili mozhna vzyat lotki naprakat.

Alice: На пля́же мо́жно игра́ть в волейбо́л?
Na plyazhi mozhna igrat v valyeibol?

Lena: Да, коне́чно. Пойдёмте.
Da, kanyeshna. Paeedyomtye.

Мо́ре так споко́йно.	The sea is so calm.
Пойдём купа́ться!	Let's go for a swim!
У вас есть купа́льный костю́м?	Have you got a swimsuit?
взять ло́дки напрока́т	to rent boats
на пля́же	on the beach

What do you like to play?

Здесь прекра́сные те́ннисные ко́рты. *Zdyes prikrasnye tennisnye korty.*	There are good tennis courts here.
Я люблю́ игра́ть в те́ннис/в хокке́й/ в футбо́л/в волейбо́л. *Ya lyooblyoo igrat v tenis/v khakhei/ v footbol/v valyeibol.*	I like playing tennis/ hockey/ soccer/volleyball.
Я люблю́ спорт/гимна́стику/ры́бную ло́влю. *Ya lyooblyoo sport/gimnastikoo/rybnuyoo lovlyoo.*	I like sports/gymnastics/ fishing.

Мóжно купáться/бéгать. *Mozhna koopatsa/byegat.*	It's possible to swim/run.
ходи́ть на лы́жах/катáться на конькáх *khadit na lyzhakh/katatsa na kankakh*	to go skiing/to go skating
катáться на трóйке/на велосипéде *katatsa na troiki/na vilasipyedi*	to go for a troika ride/ bike ride
Мóжно постáвить палáтку. *Mozhna pastavit palatkoo.*	It's possible to pitch a tent.
Я плóхо плáваю. *Ya plokha plavayoo.*	I can't swim very well.
Я не умéю игрáть в шáхматы. *Ya ni oomeyoo igrat v shakhmaty.*	I don't know how to play chess.

What can we rent?

Мóжно взять напрокáт лы́жи/коньки́/ракéтку *Mozhna vzyat naprakat lyzhi/kanki/rakyetkoo*	You can rent skis/skates/ a racket
сáни/гребнýю лóдку/пáрусную лóдку *sani/gribnuyoo lotkoo/paroosnuyoo lotkoo*	a sled/rowboat/sailboat
мячи́/вóдные лы́жи/сéрфинг *myachi/vodnye lyzhi/serfing*	balls/water skis/ a windsurfer
Скóлько стóит в час? *Skolka stoit v chas?*	How much does it cost for an hour?

The vocabulary of sports

cup	**кýбок**	*koobak*	team	**комáнда**	*kamanda*
game	**игрá**	*igra*	player	**игрóк**	*igrok*
match	**матч**	*match*	win, victory	**побéда**	*pabyeda*

Visiting the Black Sea coast The Black Sea is where Russians like to go on vacation — notably to the famous Caucasian health resort of **Sochi**, or to **Yalta**. From Yalta, you can take boat trips down the coast, or join excursions up into the mountains. A few miles along the coast is the palace of **Livadia**, once a residence of the Russian royal family, now a museum and art gallery. Trade unions and workplaces have their own vacation camps on the Black Sea for the benefit of their workers, children come here with school or Pioneer groups to summer camps, and the better-off come to spend the summer in their own dachas. Nowadays Black Sea resorts are also used for catering to foreign tourists, and the atmosphere is relaxed and friendly.

MAKING FRIENDS

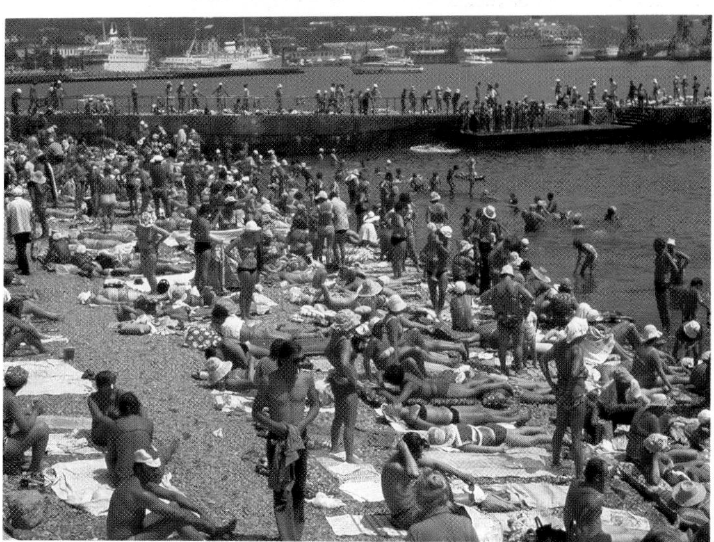

No trip to a country is complete without some kind of contact with its inhabitants. If you are on business, you will have plenty of opportunity to talk to Russians, but if you are on vacation you may have to make your own opportunities. Many Russians have studied English at school and will be glad to talk to you. If you are invited out or if you are going to visit Russian friends, it's a nice gesture to take a little gift, such as flowers. Other gifts you might like to bring from home as presents for your guide, for example, could be chocolates, cosmetics, perfume, books and magazines (nothing risqué!), records, or souvenirs.

приглашение/an invitation

The three have just arrived at the beach, when Lena unexpectedly bumps into an old friend, Olga, and her son Sasha.

Lena: О́льга, како́й сюрпри́з — и Са́шенька! Вы здесь в о́тпуске?
Olga, kakoi syoorpreez — i Sashinka! Vy zdyes v otpooski?

Olga: Да, мы отдыха́ем в Я́лте.
Da, my atdykhayem v Yalti.

Lena: Хорошо́ вам! Майк, **разреши́те предста́вить** ста́рую подру́гу. А́лис, это Са́ша. (to Olga) Майк учи́тель — ру́сского языка́.
Kharasho vam! Mike, razrishitye predstavit staruyoo padroogoo. Alice, eta Sasha. Mike — oochityel roosskava yazyka.

Olga: Вы в Я́лте в пе́рвый раз?
Vy v Yaltye v pyerviy raz?
Mike: Да, но я отдыха́л в Со́чи два го́да тому́ наза́д.
Da, no ya atdykhal v Sochi dva goda tamoo nazat.
Olga: Вам нра́вится здесь?
Vam nravitsa zdyes?
Alice: **Замеча́тельно!**
Zamichatyelna!
Olga: **Кака́я симпати́чная** де́вушка! Майк, А́лис, я **хочу́ вас пригласи́ть к себе́** на у́жин сего́дня ве́чером. Согла́сны?
Kakaya simpatichnaya dyevooshka. Mike, Alice, ya khachoo vas priglasit k sibye na oozhin sivodnya vyecheram. Saglasny?
Mike: Большо́е спаси́бо. Мы с удово́льствием придём.
Balshoye spaseeba. My s oodavolstviyem pridyom.

Making conversation

О́льга, како́й сюрпри́з! *Olga, kakoi syoorpeez!*	Olga, what a surprise!
Вы здесь в о́тпуске? — Хорошо́ вам! *Vy zdyes v otpooski? — Kharasho vam!*	Are you here on vacation — How nice for you!
Как (ва́ши) дела́? *Kak (vashi) dyela?*	How are things?
Хорошо́/норма́льно/ничего́/пло́хо. *Kharasho/narmalna/nichevo/plokha.*	Fine/OK/not bad/not too good.
Разреши́те предста́вить ста́рую подру́гу. *Razhrishitye predstavit staruyoo padroogoo.*	Let me introduce an old friend (female).
Познако́мьтесь. *Paznakomtyes.*	Let's introduce ourselves.
А́лис, это Са́ша . . . о́чень рад/ра́да/ра́ды. *Alice, eta Sasha . . . ochin rad/rada/rady.*	Alice, this is Sasha . . . pleased to meet you.
Расскажи́те о себе́. *Raskazhiti o sibye.*	Tell me about yourself.
Вы здесь в пе́рвый раз? *Vy zdyes v pyerviy raz?*	Are you here for the first time?
Отдыха́л в Крыму́ два го́да тому́ наза́д. *Atdykhal v Krymoo dva goda tamoo nazat.*	I vacationed in the Crimea 2 years ago.
Как вам нра́вится? — Замеча́тельно! *Kak vam nravitsa? — Zamichatyelna!*	How do you like it? — It's great!

Inviting someone over

Я хочу́ пригласи́ть вас к себе́ на у́жин. *Ya khachoo priglasit vas k sibye na oozhin.*	I want to invite you to supper with us.
Приходи́те к нам обе́дать/у́жинать. *Prikhaditye k nam abyedat/oozhinat.*	Come and have lunch/supper with us.
Приглаша́ю вас на вечери́нку. *Priglashayoo vas na vyecherinkoo.*	I'm inviting you to a party.
непреме́нно/согла́сны *nyeprimyenna/saglasny*	certainly/agreed
Мы придём с удово́льствием. *My pridyom s oodavolstviyem.*	We'd love to come.
Кака́я симпати́чная да́ма! *Kakaya simpatichnaya dama!*	What a nice lady!

Talking about jobs

Чем вы занима́етесь? *Chyem vy zanimaetyes?*	What do you do?
Кем вы рабо́таете? *Kyem vy rabotaetye?*	What work do you do?

If you fall into conversation with Soviet citizens, you will want to be able to say whether you're here on business (**по дела́м** *po dyelam*) or on vacation (**в о́тпуске** *v otpooski*) and what you do for a living:

Я коммерса́нт. *Ya kammirsant.*	I'm a businessman.
Я журнали́ст. *Ya zhoornalist.*	I'm a journalist.
Майк учи́тель. *Mike oochityel.*	Mike's a teacher.

See p. 115 for a list of jobs.

the way it works

I play tennis

Use the expression **игра́ть в** *igrat v* when talking about what games you play:

Я игра́ю в те́ннис, в ка́рты. *Ya igrayoo v tennis, v karty.*	I play tennis, cards.

If it's a musical instrument, you use **игра́ть на** *igrat na*:

Я игра́ю на пиани́но, на кларне́те, на скри́пке. *Ya igrayoo na pianina, na klarnyeti, na skripki.*	I play the piano, clarinet, violin.

things to do

7.1 This is something of a review exercise — look back through earlier sections if you get stuck.

You feel like a swim so you head for the swimming pool (**бассе́йн для пла́вания** *bassein dlya plavaniya*). See if you can cope with the cashier:

Вы: (You want to know how much it costs to get in)
Касси́р: Сто́ит два рубля́.
Вы: (You want to know what time the pool closes)
Касси́р: В полови́не седьмо́го.
Вы: (You didn't bring a towel — can you have one?)
Касси́р: Да, сто́ит ещё 50 копе́ек.
Вы: (Tell him you're giving him 5 rubles)
Касси́р: И вот вам сда́ча — 2 р. 50 коп. Спаси́бо.

(**сда́ча** = change)

7.2 You're interested in sports, so you go to the local sports complex and look at the list of summer events.

Летние События

Кубок Советского Союза (All-Soviet Cup)

Вечерняя гимнастика	1 АВГУСТА
ЧЕМПИОНАТ ЕВРОПЫ — Атлетика	15 АВГУСТА 14 ч.
Футбольный Матч СССР — ЧССР	22 АВГУСТА 15 ч.
БОКС — Чемпионат СССР	3 СЕНТЯБРЯ 17.30 ч.

Продажа билетов в Спортивном Комплексе

1 What could you go to on August 22?
2 You are an athletics fan. What is there to interest you?
3 At what time of day can you see gymnastics?
4 What other championship is going to be on, and when?
5 Where can you get tickets for these events?

7.3 Here are some of the things you and your friends would like to rent during your leisure time in the Soviet Union. Practice asking for them, and asking how much they will cost.

1 

2 

3 

4 

7.4 You and a friend are sitting at a cafe on the sea front, and fall into conversation with a Russian lady at the next table. Can you make yourself understood? You have indicated that you're English. Now continue . . .

Дама: Вы англича́не, вот интере́сно. Где вы живёте в А́нглии?
Вы: (You're from London.)
Дама: Как вам нра́вится Крым? Здесь жа́рко, не пра́вда ли?
Вы: (You like it very much, and yes, it's very hot.)
Дама: Скажи́те, кем вы рабо́таете?
Вы: (Tell her what you do, e.g., you're a teacher and your friend is a doctor.)

GOING ON AN EXCURSION

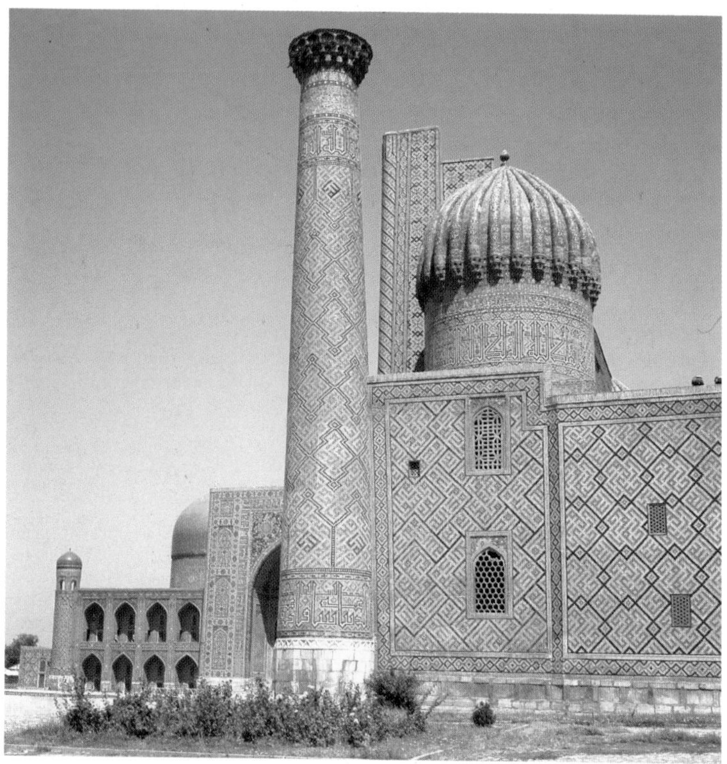

If you are on an organized tour, you will be taken on at least one sightseeing tour, and will have the opportunity of joining the various excursions that are available in the Soviet Union. Excursions can only be undertaken with special permission, so if there is anything you particularly want to see, you should arrange it in writing beforehand, or apply to the service bureau at your hotel for advice.

There are many churches in the Soviet Union, and most of them are open to the public. The majority are now museums and have been beautifully restored or maintained. The country is proud of its ancient monuments and historic buildings and looks after them with care — visitors should do the same. In the churches in which services (**слу́жба** *sloozhba*) are still held, you should behave respectfully, and women should wear headscarves.

экскурсия в древний город/an excursion to an ancient town

Samarkand, once capital of the Mongol Empire, is a feast for the eye with its glorious mosques and many blue-tiled domes. Visitors flock to see the mausoleum of Gur Emir, Bibi-Khanym's Mosque, and the picture-book buildings of the Registan — once a theological college, now a showpiece of Eastern-style architecture.

Lucy and her fellow travelers have arrived in Samarkand and spent the morning looking around the Registan complex. Vadim reminds them that an excursion has been planned for the afternoon . . .

Vadim: Сего́дня больша́я экску́рсия в дре́вний го́род, недалеко́ от Самарка́нда. Вы мо́жете посмотре́ть чуде́сные минаре́ты, мече́ть четы́рнадцатого ве́ка с си́ней черепи́цей, мавзоле́й и па́мятники дре́вней узбе́кской архитекту́ры. Авто́бус отправля́ется в два часа́. Э́то вам подхо́дит?
Sivodnya balshaya ekskursiya v drevniy gorat, nidalyeko at Samarkanda. Vy mozhetye pasmatryet choodyesnye minarety, michet chetyrnatsatava vyeka s sinyei chirepitsei, mavzolei i pamyatniki drevnei oozbekskoi arkhitektoory. Avtoboos atpravlyaitsa v dva chasa. Eta vam padkhodit?

Lucy: Да, восто́чная архитекту́ра — очарова́тельна. Я должна́ вста́вить плёнку в фотоаппара́т.
Da, vastochnaya arkhitektoora — acharavatilna. Ya dulzhna vstavit plyonkoo v fotaapparat.

мече́ть	mosque
век	century
с си́ней черепи́цей	with blue tiles
па́мятники дре́вней узбе́кской архитекту́ры	monuments of ancient Uzbek architecture
восто́чная	Eastern
вста́вить плёнку в	put a roll of film in

They arrive at the ancient city, and enter a mosque. Lucy is fascinated by the decorated ceiling, and the costumes of some of the women standing by the door.

Lucy: Какóй удиви́тельный потолóк, и каки́е прекрáсные костю́мы! **Я должнá дéлать сни́мки.**
Kakoi oodivityelniy patalok, i kakiye prekrasnye kastyoomy! Ya dulzhna dyelat snimki.

(She gets out her camera and takes aim . . .)

Woman: Нельзя́ фотографи́ровать, как вам не сты́дно!
Nilzya fatagrafiravat, kak vam ni stydna!

Lucy: (Taken aback) Виновáта, прости́те меня́.
Vinavata, prastitye minya.

Vadim: Э́то не вáжно, Лю́си. Порá обрáтно — пойдём вы́пьем чтó-нибудь в гости́нице.
Eta ni vazhna, Lucy. Para abratna — paeedyom, vypyem shto-niboot v gastinitsi!

Как вам не сты́дно!	Aren't you ashamed!	**Виновáта.**	I'm sorry (fem.).
прости́те меня́	excuse me	**Не вáжно.**	It's not important.
Порá обрáтно.	It's time to get back.		

Taking a trip

Сегóдня экскýрсия в дрéвний гóрод. *Sivodnya ekskoorsiya v drevniy gorat.*	Today there's an excursion to an ancient town.
в Бухарý/Петродворéц/Кремль *v Bookharoo/Petradvaryets/Kreml*	to Bukhara/Petrodvorets/ the Kremlin
посещéние музéя *pasyeshcheniye moozeya*	a visit to the museum
Вы мóжете посмотрéть чудéсные минарéты. *Vy mozhetye pasmatryet choodyesnye minarety.*	You can see wonderful minarets.
мечéть четы́рнадцатого вéка, мавзолéй *michet chityrnatsatovo vyeka, mavzolei*	a 14th-century mosque, a mausoleum
посмотрéть Москвý/Ки́ев/Новосиби́рск *pasmatryet Maskvoo/Kiev/Navasibirsk*	look at Moscow/Kiev/ Novosibirsk
Мóжно осмотрéть все достопримечáтельности. *Mozhna asmatryet vsye dastaprimichatilnasti.*	You can see all the sights.

Авто́бус отправля́ется в два часа́. *Avtoboos atpravlyaitsa v dva chasa.*	The coach sets off at 2 o'clock.
Это вам подхо́дит? *Eta vam padkhodit?*	Does that suit you?
Восто́чная архитекту́ра очарова́тельна. *Vastochnaya arkhitektoora acharavatyelna.*	Eastern architecture is fascinating.
Како́й удиви́тельный потоло́к. *Kakoi oodivityelniy patalok.*	What an amazing ceiling.

For a list of places to see and things to look at, see p. 116.

TAKING PHOTOGRAPHS

Be careful how you aim your camera, as there are quite a number of places you are not allowed to photograph in the Soviet Union, among them airports, stations, military buildings, etc., aerial views (e.g., from the top of a church or tower), bridges, border areas, industrial installations, and the inside of shops and churches. Don't try to take snapshots of people in uniform or buildings where there is a uniformed guard. People at work generally don't like to be photographed, whether driving a bus or cleaning a building, and if you want to take a picture of someone, it is polite to ask for permission: **Мо́жно вас фотографи́ровать?** *Mozhna vas fatagrafiravat?* You can now buy color film in some Beriozka shops, but as 35 mm film is not readily available it is best to take your own supply.

I must take a photo!

You'll want to take photos as a reminder of your trip, but don't do what Lucy did — remember to ask first!

плёнка, цветна́я позити́вная *plyonka, tsvitnaya pazitivnaya*	film, color slide
Я должна́ вста́вить плёнку в фотоаппара́т *Ya dulzhna vstavit plyonkoo v fotaapparat*	I must put a roll of film in my camera
. . . де́лать сни́мки *. . . dyelat snimki*	. . . take some snapshots
Нельзя́ фотографи́ровать. *Nilzya fatagrafirovat.*	You can't take a photo.
ФОТОГРАФИ́РОВАТЬ ЗАПРЕЩА́ЕТСЯ *Fatagrafiravat zaprishchaitsa*	NO PHOTOGRAPHS

Nouns and adjectives in Russian and how they work: a review

	masc. sing.		*masc. plural*	
Nominative:	белый стол	рубль	новые столы	рубли
Accusative:	белый стол	рубль	новые столы	рубли
Genitive:	белого стола	рубля	новых столов	рублей
Dative:	белому столу	рублю́	новым столам	рублям
Instrumental:	белым столом	рублём	новыми столами	рублями
Locative:	белом столе	рубле	новых столах	рублях

	fem. sing.			*fem. plural*		
Nominative:	старая страна	дверь	земля	страны	двери	земли
Accusative:	старую страну	дверь	землю	страны	двери	земли
Genitive:	старой страны	двери	земли	стран	дверей	земель
Dative:	старой стране	двери	земле	странам	дверям	землям
Instrumental:	старой страной	дверью	землёй	странами	дверями	землями
Locative:	старой стране	двери	земле	странах	дверях	землях

	neuter sing.		*neuter plural*	
Nominative:	новое место	поле	места	поля
Accusative:	новое место	поле	места	поля
Genitive:	нового места	поля	мест	полей
Dative:	новому месту	полю	местам	полям
Instrumental:	новым местом	полем	местами	полями
Locative:	новом месте	поле	местах	полях

Most nouns and adjectives in Russian follow patterns similar to these (remember that after **г, к, х, ж, ч, ш,** and **щ, ы** become **и**).

things to do

7.5 You had a memorable time in the USSR. You're back home and putting away some papers, when you come across the itinerary for your trip. Here is the relevant page from your diary. Can you still remember it all . . .?

РАСПИСАНИЕ ПОЕЗДКИ

Пн.	Прибытие в Москву Посещение города — Кремль, Мавзолей Ленина
Вт.	Конференция
Ср.	Конференция Посещение ВДНХ*
Чт.	Экскурсия в Архангельское цена 25 р.
Пт.	Конференция Экскурсия в монастырь 14-ого века ц. 15 р.
Сб.	Свободный день Вечеринка 20 ч.
Вс.	Отправление 12 ч. Москва-Шереметьево

***ВДНХ**: (Permanent) Exhibition of Economic Achievements of the USSR.

ВОСКРЕСЕНЬЕ SUNDAY

Mon	Exhausting day, but memorable. Used up a whole film!
Tues	Hard at work today – made quite a few contacts.
Wed	Beginning to get settled in. Particulary impressed by afternoon visit
Thurs	A great day out. Made a new friend on the coach!
Fri	Last day on official business. Once again, interesting afternoon.
Sat	Went shopping, bought lots of presents and spent far too much money. The vodka flowed well into the night!
Sun	Flight was late, I think. Can't remember much about today...

1 Why was Monday so exhausting, and what did you take pictures of?
2 What did you have to do on Tuesday, Wednesday, and Friday?
3 Where did you go on Thursday? Was it free, or did you have to pay?
4 What excursion was available on Friday afternoon?
5 What was arranged for Saturday? What was arranged for the evening?
6 What time did you leave Moscow on Sunday?

KEY TO EXERCISES

Before you leave 1 *kamyeta* (comet), *kafé* (café), *bolt* (bolt), *dama* (lady), *fakt* (fact), *kofi* (coffee), *balyet* (ballet), *mama* (mom), *ballada* (ballad), *takt* (tact), *foto* (photo), *koma* (coma), *tabak* (tobacco), *data* (data), *blok* (bloc), *katlyeta* (cutlet), *atam* (atom), *kadyet* (cadet). 2 *da, kto, eta, tyela, dom, kak, malako, moda, dyela, tam, tak, mala.* 3 *Taksi* (taxi), *tilifon* (telephone), *vistibyool* (vestibule), *traktor* (tractor), *park* (park), *viza* (visa), *toorist* (tourist), *tsentr* (center), *klinik* (clinic), *boofyet* (buffet), *dinama* (dynamo), *kantsert* (concert), *film* (film), *bank* (bank), *mitro* (metro), *vino* (wine), *vodka* (vodka), *twalyet* (toilet), *stoodyent* (student), *gazyeta* (newspaper).

1.1 1 *ristaran* — restaurant
2 *intoorist* — Intourist
3 *sooveniry* — souvenirs
4 *kassa* — cashier
1.2 1 Здравствуйте. Очень приятно. 2 Добрый день. 3 Доброе утро. 4 До свидания.
1.3 2 Да, я мистер Наш. 3 Да, меня зовут Кларк. 4 Нет, меня зовут Томпсон. 5 Я Анна Блак/Меня зовут Анна Блак.
1.4 1 (Триста) пять, восемь и десять. 2 (Извините, пожалуйста) Где ванная? 3 Принесите мне полотенце.
1.5. On the first floor; the snack bar.
1.6. *kantora, zvanok, moozhskoi, zhenskiy.*
1.7 1 У вас есть чай с лимоном? 2 Дайте кофе и яблочный сок. 3 Бутылка лимонада, пожалуйста. Спасибо.
1.8 Чашка кофе и стакан чая, пожалуйста./(Чай) Без сахара./У вас есть томатный сок?/Спасибо, нет. Дайте фруктовый сок, пожалуйста./ Да, это всё. Спасибо.

2.1 Fried eggs, jam.
2.2 Я возьму/Дайте омлет./Омлет с ветчиной./Чай, пожалуйста.
2.3 английская . . . стоит . . . рубль . . . копеек . . . журнал . . . американский . . . карту . . . по-русски . . . рубля. (Customer/News/vendor: Good afternoon. Have you got an English paper?/Yes, I've got *The Times*./ How much is it?/1 ruble 20 kopecks./I want to buy an English magazine, too./I'm very sorry (I haven't got one). We've got an American magazine — *Time*./Give me a map of Leningrad./A map in Russian or in English?/In Russian, thank you./2 rubles 10 kopecks.
2.4 1 Стоит два рубля двадцать пять копеек. 2 Стоит один рубль десять копеек. 3 Стоит пятьдесят копеек. 4 Стоит два рубля пять копеек.
2.5 *Kafé-Marozhenaye, Shashlychnaya, Zakoosachnaya.*
2.6 Woman: Красная икра, баранина с рисом, компот. Man: Щи, котлеты по-киевски, ванильное мороженое. Man: Салат из помидоров, гуляш с картофелем, сыр. Lucy: Осетрина, свинина с грибами, кисель.
2.7 Принесите/Дайте бутылку красного вина, бутылку белого вина, джин с тоником, светлое пиво и водку.

3.1 *Vkhod, Vykhad, Zapasnoi Vykhad, Vkhoda nyet, Vykhada nyet.*
3.2 3.
3.3 0:30 a.m.; 12:30 p.m.; 17:40 p.m. Это прямой поезд.
3.4 Это место занято?/Можно открыть окно?/(Когда) В котором часу приходит поезд в Киев? /Пожалуйста, где вагон-ресторан?
3.5 1 В Лондоне, половина первого; в Москве, половина четвёртого. 2 В Москве, четверть двенадцатого; в Иркутске, четверть пятого. 3 В Нью-Йорке, пять часов; в Ленинграде, час. 4 В Ялте, без четверти семь; в Ташкенте, без четверти девять.

3.6 *stoitye* (wait, lit. stand), *iditye* (cross, lit. go), *stop* (stop), *pirikhod* (crossing), *byeregis aftamabilya* (beware of cars).
3.7 (a) e.g. 1 Пожалуйста, где кино? 2 Как пройти в гостиницу? Где находится стадион?
(b) 1 Bank. 2 Art gallery.
3 Museum
3.8 Hotel National, Lenin Museum, Red Square.

4.1 *Kievskaya, Arbatskaya, Krapotkinskaya. Biblioteka im. (imyeni) Lenina, Ploshchad Sverdlova; apoostitye pyat kapeyek* — insert 5 kop., *k payezdam* — to the trains, *vykhad v gorat* — exit to the town.
4.2 (a) 3, (b) 5, (c) 4, (d) 2, (e) 1.
4.3 1 Извините пожалуйста, где станция метро? 2 Извините пожалуйста, (вы не знаете) где станция Проспект Мира?
3 Пожалуйста, где остановка троллейбуса? 4 В театр, пожалуйста. 5 Сорок литров, пожалуйста.
4.4 *foyé* (foyer), *kooritelnaya komnata* (smoking room), *v kino nilzya koorit* (no smoking in the movie theater), *administrator* (manager).
4.5 1. Yes. 2 Yes. 3 Mondays.
4.6 1. June 13th, 1989. 2. Dress circle, on the left. 3. Row 8, seat 5.
4.7 1 Два билета на балконе на завтра. 2 В котором часу начинается спектакль/представление? 3 Один билет в партере — середина — на сегодня (вечером). 4 У вас есть места на сегодняшний концерт? 5 У меня осталось только билеты на седьмое февраля.

5.1 1 Можно обменять американские доллары? 2 Можно обменять двадцать пять фунтов? 3 Здесь можно разменять дорожные чеки?
4 Какой сегодня курс?
5.2 (b).
5.3 (c).
5.4 мороженое — два, пожалуйста; фруктовый сок — четыре, пожалуйста; билет — шесть, пожалуйста; открытки — десять, пожалуйста.
5.5 5 rubles 10 kopecks (пять рублей десять копеек).
5.6 (Дайте) Батон, пожалуйста./Две булочки и пирожное.
5.7 Покажите пожалуйста зелёную рубашку в витрине./Нет, не эту, а ту, рядом . . . Сколько она стоит?/Нет, не надо — она слишком дорога.
5.8 1 (c), 2 (d), 3 (a), 4 (e), 5 (b).
5.9 1 Пластинка (the record).
2 Открытки (the postcards).
3 Книга (the book).
4 Счёт (the abacus)
5.10 (a) Сувениры
(b) & (c) Поднос, десять рублей двадцать пять копеек; шаль, восемь рублей пятьдесят копеек; часы, семьдесят пять рублей; матрёшка, шестнадцать рублей тридцать копеек.

6.1 У меня болит желудок./Да, у меня болит голова, и меня тошнит. Diagnosis: sunstroke.
6.2 1 У неё болит нога. 2 У него болит спина. 3 У неё несварение желудка. 4 У него укус насекомого 5 У неё простуда.
6.3 1 Вата, таблетки для горла, средство от комаров. 2 Зубная паста, мыло и лезвия. 3 У вас есть что-нибудь от поноса?
6.4 Бутерброд с сыром; бутерброд с икрой; пирог с мясом; сырники.
6.5 1 Сколько стоит письмо в США? 2 Две марки за пятьдесят копеек. 3 Дайте мне/Где международный бланк? 4 Заверните, пожалуйста. Сколько стоит (посылка)?
6.6 1 You're wanted on the phone. 2 Нет, это . . . (your name)/ Это ошибка. 3 Hold the line a minute.
6.7 Сумочку; фотоаппарат; паспорт; багаж; деньги.

7.1 Пожалуйста, сколько стоит билет?/В котором часу закрывается бассейн?/(У вас есть) Можно взять напрокат полотенце?/Вот (вам) пять рублей.
7.2 1 Soccer match (USSR v. Czechoslovakia). 2 European championship on August 15. 3 In the evening. 4 Boxing, on September 3rd at 5:30 pm 5 At the sports complex.
7.3 Я хочу/хотел бы/хотела бы взять напрокат гребную лодку. . . коньки. . . ракетку и мячи. . . серфинг. Сколько стоит?
7.4 (Я) Мы из Лондона./(Мне) нам очень нравится. Да, очень жарко./e.g. Я — учитель, мой друг (моя подруга) — врач.
7.5 1 You arrived in Moscow and then went on a visit of the city. You took pictures, among other things, of the Kremlin and Lenin's tomb. 2 You attended a conference. 3 You went to Archangelskoye and it cost you 25 rubles. 4 An excursion to a 14th-century monastery. 5 It was a free day, with a party arranged for the evening. 6 You left at 12 noon.

VOCABULARY

Some common verbs in Russian

дава́ть to give

я даю́	*ya dayoo*	I give	мы даём	*my dayom*	we give
ты даёшь	*ty dayosh*	you give	вы даёте	*vy dayotye*	you give
он даёт	*on dayot*	he gives	они́ даю́т	*ani dayoot*	they give

ви́деть to see

я ви́жу	*ya vizhoo*	I see	мы ви́дим	*my vidim*	we see
ты ви́дишь	*ty vidish*	you see	вы ви́дите	*vy viditye*	you see
он ви́дит	*on vidit*	he sees	они́ ви́дят	*ani vidyat*	they see

хоте́ть to want

я хочу	*ya khachoo*	I want	мы хоти́м	*my khatim*	we want
ты хо́чешь	*ty khochesh*	you want	вы хоти́те	*vy khatitye*	you want
он хоче́т	*on khochet*	he wants	они́ хотя́т	*ani khatyat*	they want

жить to live, stay (in a hotel)

я живу́	*ya zhivoo*	I live	мы живём	*my zhivyom*	we live
ты живёшь	*ty zhivyosh*	you live	вы живёте	*vy zhivyotye*	you live
он живёт	*on zhivyot*	he lives	они́ живу́т	*ani zhivoot*	they live

мочь to be able

я могу́	*ya magoo*	I can	мы мо́жем	*my mozhem*	we can
ты мо́жешь	*ty mozhesh*	you can	вы мо́жете	*vy mozhetye*	you can
он мо́жет	*on mozhet*	he can	они́ мо́гут	*ani mogoot*	they can

люби́ть to like, to love

я люблю́	*ya lyooblyoo*	I love	мы лю́бим	*my lyoobim*	we love
ты лю́бишь	*ty lyoobish*	you love	вы лю́бите	*vy lyoobitye*	you love
он лю́бит	*on lyoobit*	he loves	они́ лю́бят	*ani lyoobyat*	they love

писа́ть to write

я пишу́	*ya pishoo*	I write	мы пи́шем	*my pishim*	we write
ты пи́шешь	*ty pishish*	you write	вы пи́шете	*vy pishitye*	you write
он пи́шет	*on pishit*	he writes	они́ пи́шут	*ani pishoot*	they write

пить to drink

я пью	*ya pyoo*	I drink	мы пьём	*my pyom*	we drink
ты пьёшь	*ty pyosh*	you drink	вы пьёте	*vy pyotye*	you drink
он пьёт	*on pyot*	he drinks	они́ пьют	*ani pyoot*	they drink

есть to eat

я ем	*ya yem*	I eat	мы еди́м	*my yedim*	we eat
ты ешь	*ty yesh*	you eat	вы еди́те	*vy yeditye*	you eat
он ест	*on yest*	he eats	они́ едя́т	*ani yedyat*	they eat

past tense: ел, е́ло, е́ла, е́ли

искать to look for

я ищу́	*ya ishchoo*	I look for	мы и́щем	*my ishchem*	we look for
ты и́щешь	*ty ishchesh*	you look for	вы и́щете	*vy ishchetye*	you look for
он и́щет	*on ishchet*	he looks for	они́ и́щут	*ani ishchoot*	they look for

English-Russian Topic Vocabularies

Numbers **(Чи́сла *Chisla*)**

Cardinal numbers 21–1000

21	**два́дцать оди́н** *dvatsat adin*	200	**две́сти** *dvyesti*
25	**два́дцать пять** *dvatsat pyat*	300	**три́ста** *trista*
30	**три́дцать** *tritsat*	400	**четы́реста** *chitirista*
40	**со́рок** *sorak*	500	**пятьсо́т** *pyatsot*
50	**пятьдеся́т** *pyatdisyat*	600	**шестьсо́т** *shestsot*
60	**шестьдеся́т** *shestdisyat*	700	**семьсо́т** *syemsot*
70	**се́мьдесять** *syemdisyat*	800	**восемьсо́т** *vosyemsot*
80	**во́семьдесят** *vosyemdisyat*	900	**девятьсо́т** *dyevyatsot*
90	**девяно́сто** *dyevyanosta*	1000	**ты́сяча** *tysyacha*
100	**сто** *sto*		

The numbers 1–20 are given on p. 7.

Ordinal numbers 1st–20th

1st	**пе́рвый** *perviy*	11th	**оди́ннадцатый** *adinnatsatiy*
2nd	**второ́й** *ftaroi*	12th	**двена́дцатый** *dvinatsatiy*
3rd	**тре́тий** *tretiy*	13th	**трина́дцатый** *trinatsatiy*
4th	**четвёртый** *chitviortiy*	14th	**четы́рнадцатый** *chitirnatsatiy*
5th	**пя́тый** *pyatiy*	15th	**пятна́дцатый** *pitnatsatiy*
6th	**шесто́й** *shestoi*	16th	**шестна́дцатый** *shesnatsatiy*
7th	**седьмо́й** *syedmoi*	17th	**семна́дцатый** *syemnatsatiy*
8th	**восьмо́й** *vasmoi*	18th	**восемна́дцатый** *vosyemnatsatiy*
9th	**девя́тый** *devyatiy*	19th	**девятна́дцатый** *divyatnatsatiy*
10th	**деся́тый** *desyatiy*	20th	**двадца́тый** *dvatsatiy*

The date **(Число́ *Chislo*)**

January	**янва́рь** *yanvar*	July	**ию́ль** *iyool*
February	**февра́ль** *fevral*	August	**а́вгуст** *avgoost*
March	**март** *mart*	September	**сентя́брь** *sentyabr*
April	**апре́ль** *aprel*	October	**октя́брь** *aktyabr*
May	**май** *mai*	November	**ноя́брь** *noyabr*
June	**ию́нь** *iyoon*	December	**дека́брь** *dekabr*

Use the neuter ending for dates:

March 1st	**пе́рвое ма́рта**
June 5th	**пя́тое ию́ня**

Public Holidays

1 January	**(пе́рвое января́)**	New Year's Day
8 March	**(восьмо́е ма́рта)**	Women's Day
1 & 2 May	**(пе́рвое и второ́е ма́я)**	May Day
9 May	**(девя́тое ма́я)**	Victory Day
7 October	**(седьмо́е октября́)**	Constitution Day
7 & 8 November	**(седьмо́е и восьмо́е ноября́)**	October Revolution Days

Food

Meat (**Мя́со** ***Myasa***)

beef **говя́дина** *guvyadina*
chicken **ку́рица** *kooritsa*
duck **у́тка** *ootka*
goose **гусь** *goos*
kidneys **по́чки** *pochki*
lamb **бара́нина** *baranina*
liver **печёнка** *pichonka*
pork **свини́на** *svinina*
steak **антреко́т** *antrecot*
turkey **инде́йка** *indeika*
veal **теля́тина** *tilyatina*

Fish (**Ры́ба** ***Ryba***)

assorted fish **ры́бная заку́ска** *rybnaya zakooska*
carp **карп** *karp*
caviar **икра́** *ikra*
cod **треска́** *triska*
crab **краб** *krab*
herring **сельдь** *syeld*
pike **щу́ка** *shchooka*
pike perch **суда́к** *soodak*
trout **форе́ль** *faryel*
salmon **сёмга** *syomga*
лосо́сь *lasos*
sprats **шпро́ты** *shproty*
sturgeon **осетри́на** *asyetrina*

Vegetables (**О́вощи** ***Ovashchi***)

beans **фасо́ль** *fasol*
cabbage **капу́ста** *kapoosta*
carrots **морко́вь** *markov*
cauliflower **цветна́я капу́ста** *tsvitnaya kapoosta*
cucumber **огуре́ц** *agooryets*
mushrooms **грибы́** *griby*
onion **лук** *look*
peas **горо́х** *garokh*
radish **реди́ска** *rediska*
salad **сала́т** *salat*
tomatoes **помидо́ры** *pamidory*

Fruit (**Фру́кты** ***Frookty***)

apple **я́блоко** *yablaka*
banana **бана́н** *banan*
cherries **ви́шни** *vishni*
grapes **виногра́д** *vinagrad*
grapefruit **гре́йпфрут** *grapefroot*
lemon **лимо́н** *limon*
melon **ды́ня** *dynya*
orange **апельси́н** *apilseen*
peach **пе́рсик** *persik*
pear **гру́ша** *groosha*
plum **сли́ва** *sliva*
raspberry **мали́на** *malina*
strawberry **клубни́ка** *kloobnika*

Groceries (**Бакале́йные това́ры** ***Bakalyeinye tavary***)

butter **ма́сло** *masla*
canned goods **консе́рвы** *kanservy*
cheese **сыр** *syr*
coffee **ко́фе** *kofi*
(without chicory) **без цико́рия** *byez tsikoriya*
cookies **пече́нье** *pichyenye*
cream **сли́вки** *slivki (pl.)*
flour **мука́** *mooka*
lard **жир** *zhir*
margarine **маргари́н** *margarin*
rice **рис** *rees*
sugar **са́хар** *sakhar*
tea **чай** *chai*

Car parts (**Дета́ли маши́ны** ***Detaly mashiny***)

accelerator **акселера́тор** *aksyelerator*
battery **батаре́я** *batareya*
brakes **тормоза́** *tarmaza*
clutch **сцепле́ние** *stsipleniye*
engine **мото́р** *mator*
exhaust **выхлопна́я труба́** *vykhlapnaya trooba*
headlights **фа́ры** *fary*
horn **гудо́к** *goodok*
ignition **зажига́ние** *zazhiganiye*
spark plugs **све́чи** *svechi*
tire **ши́на** *shina*
turn signals **указа́тели поворо́та** *ookazateli pavarota*
(steering) wheel **(рулево́е) колесо́** *(roolevoye kaliso)*
wheels **колёса** *kalyosa*

windshield wipers	**стеклоочисти́тели** *stikla-achistitili*
spare parts	**запча́сти** *zapchasti*

Clothes (**Оде́жда** ***Adyezhda***)

bathing suit	**купа́льный костю́м** *koopalniy kastyoom*
belt	**по́яс** *poyas*
blouse	**блу́зка** *bloozka*
boots	**сапоги́** *sapagi*
bra	**ли́фчик** *leefchik*
briefs	**тру́сики** *troosiki*
cardigan	**шерстяно́й дже́мпер** *sherstyanoi dzhemper*
coat	**пальто́** *palto*
dress	**пла́тье** *platye*
fur coat	**шу́ба** *shooba*
gloves	**перча́тки** *pirchatki*
hat	**шля́па** *shlyapa*
jacket	**пиджа́к** *pidzhak*
jeans	**джи́нсы** *dzhinsy*
raincoat	**плащ** *plashch*
scarf	**шарф** *sharf*
shirt	**руба́шка** *roobashka*
shoes	**ту́фли** *toofli*
skirt	**ю́бка** *yoopka*
socks	**носки́** *naski*
stockings	**чулки́** *choolki*
sweater	**сви́тер** *sviter*
sweatshirt	**спорти́вный свитер** *spartivniy sviter*
tie	**га́лстук** *galstook*
tights	**колго́тки** *kalgotki*
T-shirt	**ма́йка** *maika*
underpants	**кальсо́ны** *kalsony*

Parts of the body (**Ча́сти те́ла** ***Chasti tyela***)

arm	**рука́** *rooka*
back	**спина́** *spina*
blood	**кровь** *krov*
bone	**кость** *kost*
chest	**грудь** *groot*
ear(s)	**у́хо, у́ши** *ookha, ooshi*
elbow	**ло́коть** *lokat*
eye(s)	**глаз, глаза́** *glaz, glaza*
face	**лицо́** *litso*
finger	**па́лец** *palyets*
foot	**нога́** *naga*
forehead	**лоб** *lop*
hair	**во́лосы** *volasy*
hand	**рука́** *rooka*
head	**голова́** *galava*
knee	**коле́но** *kalyena*
leg	**нога́** *naga*
mouth	**рот** *rot*
neck	**ше́я** *sheya*
nose	**нос** *nos*
shoulder	**плечо́** *plicho*
stomach	**желу́док** *zheloodak*
throat	**го́рло** *gorla*
toe	**па́лец на ноге́** *palyets na nagye*
tooth	**зуб** *zoop*

Toiletries (**Предме́ты туале́та** ***Predmyety twalyeta***)

brush	**щётка** *shchotka*
cologne	**одеколо́н** *adikalon*
comb	**гре́бень** *gryebin*
diapers	**пелёнки** *pilyonki*
face cream	**крем для лица́** *krem dlya litsa*
hand cream	**крем для рук** *krem dlya rook*
perfume	**духи́** *dookhi*
powder	**пу́дра** *poodra*
razor	**бри́тва** *britva*
shaving cream	**крем для бритья́** *krem dlya britya*
soap	**мы́ло** *myla*
suntan oil	**ма́сло для зага́ра** *masla dlya zagara*
toothbrush	**зубна́я щётка** *zoobnaya shchotka*
toothpaste	**зубна́я па́ста** *zoobnaya pasta*
shampoo	**шампу́нь** *shampoon*

Jobs (**Профе́ссии** ***Prafesii***)

accountant	**бухга́лтер** *bookhgalter*
artist	**худо́жник** *khoodozhnik*
businessman	**коммерса́нт** *kammirsant*
chef	**по́вар** *povar*
doctor	**врач** *vrach*
economist	**экономи́ст** *ekanamist*

engineer	**инженéр** *inzhenyer*
hairdresser	**парикмáхер** *parikmakher*
journalist	**журналúст** *zhoornalist*
lawyer	**адвокáт** *advakat*
mathematician	**математик** *matematik*
mechanic	**механик** *mekhanik*
nurse	**медсестрá** *myedsistra*
pensioner	**пенсионéр(ка)** *pensioner(ka)*
programmer	**программúст** *programmist*
salesman	**продавéц** *prodavyets*
saleswoman	**продавщúца** *prodavshchitsa*
student	**студéнт(ка)** *stoodyent(ka)*
teacher	**учúтель, -ница** *oochityel, -nitsa*
writer	**писáтель, -ница** *pisatyel, -nitsa*

Things to see **(Достопримечáтельности *Dastaprimichatilnasti*)**

archeology	**археолóгия** *arkhealogiya*
architecture	**архитектýра** *arkhitektoora*
art	**искýсство** *iskoosstva*
castle	**зáмок** *zamak*
cemetery	**клáдбище** *kladbishche*
exhibition	**вы́ставка** *vystavka*
fortress	**крéпость** *krepast*
gardens	**сады́** *sady*
monastery	**монасты́рь** *manastyr*
palace	**дворéц** *dvaryets*
park	**парк** *park*
ruins	**развáлины** *razvaliny*
tomb	**могúла** *magila*

Russian-English Vocabulary

а *a* and, but
авиаписьмó *aviapismo* airmail letter
автóбус *aftoboos* bus
америкáнец *amerikanyets* (m.) American
америкáнка *amerikanka* (f.) American
америкáнский/ая/ое/ие *amerikanskiy/aya/aye/iye* (adj.) American
Áнглия *Angliya* England
англúйский/ая/ое/ие *angliiskiy/aya/aye/iye* (adj.) English
англичáнин/-чáнка *anglichanin/-chanka* Englishman/woman
аптéка *aptyeka* pharmacy
атлéтика *atlyetika* athletics
аэропóрт *aeroport* airport

бáбушка *babooshka* grandmother
багáж *bagazh* luggage
бакалéя *bakaleya* grocery; groceries
балéт *balyet* ballet
банк *bank* bank
бар *bar* bar
бассéйн для плáвания *bassein dlya plavaniya* swimming pool
без *byez* without, minus
бéлый/ая/ое/ые *byely/aya/aye/ye* white
бензúн *benzin* gasoline
беспокóить *byespakoit* disturb; **-ся** *-sa* worry
библиотéка *bibliotyeka* library
билéт *bilyet* ticket
ближáйший/ая/ее/ие *blizhaishiy/aya/yeye/iye* nearest
блúнчик *blinchik* pancake
блýзка *bloozka* blouse
блю́до *blyooda* dish, course

VOCABULARY

боли́т: у меня́ — *balit: oo minya* — my ... hurts
боль *bol* pain
больни́ца *balnitsa* hospital
бо́льше ничего́ *bolshe nichevo* nothing else
большо́й/а́я/о́е/и́е *balshoi/aya/oye/iye* large, big
бу́дет *boodyet* (there) will be; **вы бу́дете...?** *vy booditye...?* will you have...?
бу́лочка *boolachka* roll
бу́лочная *boolachnaya* baker
бума́га *boomaga* paper
бума́жник *boomazhnik* wallet
бутербро́д *booterbrod* sandwich
буты́лка *bootylka* bottle
бюро́ *byoora* office; — **нахо́док** — *nakhodak* lost and found — **обслу́живания** —*apsloozhivaniya* service bureau
бы́стро *bystra* quick(ly)
быть *byt* to be

в *v* in, at, to
ваго́н *vagon* carriage; **спа́льный** — *spalniy vagon* sleeping car; — **- рестора́н** — *-ristaran* dining car
валю́та *valyoota* (foreign) currency
ва́нная *vannaya* bathroom
варе́нье *varenye* jam
ваш/ва́ша/ва́ше/ва́ши *vash/vasha/vashe/vashi* (adj.) your
вероя́тно *verayatna* probably
весь/вся/всё/все *vyes/vsya/vsyo/vsye* (adj.) all
ветчина́ *vetchina* ham
ве́чер *vyecher* evening; **-ом** *-am* in the evening
вечери́нка *vyecherinka* party
взять напрока́т *vzyat naprakat* rent
ви́деть *vidyet* see; **я ви́жу** *ya vizhoo* I see
вино́ *vino* wine
винова́т/а *vinavat/a* (adj. m/f.) sorry (guilty)
виногра́д *vinagrad* grapes
витри́на *vitrina* (shop) window
вку́сный/ая/ое/ые *fkoosniy/aya/aye/ye* tasty
вода́ *vada* water
во́дка *vodka* vodka
возьму: я́ — *vazmoo: ya* — I'll have (take)
вокза́л *vagzal* station
вон там *von tam* over there
вот *vot* here's/there's, here it is, etc.
врач *vrach* doctor
вре́мя *vremya* time
всегда́ *fsikda* always
вход *vkhod* entrance
вчера́ *fchera* yesterday
вы/вас/вам/ва́ми *vy/vas/vam/vami* you
вы́пишите! *vipishitye!* Write (it) out!
высо́кий/ая/ое/ие *vysokiy/aya/aye/iye* high
вы́ставка *vystavka* exhibition
вы́ход *vykhad* exit

газе́та *gazyeta* newspaper
галере́я *galireya* gallery
гардеро́б *gardirob* cloakroom
где *gdye* where
гид *geed* guide
говори́ть *gavarit* speak
год *god* year; **два -а тому́ наза́д** *dva -a tamoo nazat* 2 years ago
годи́тся: э́то — *gaditsa: eta* — it will do
голова́ *galava* head
голо́дный/ая/ое/ые *galodniy/aya/aye/ye* hungry
го́рло *gorla* throat
го́род *gorat* town
горя́чий/ая/ее/ие *garyachiy/aya/eye/iye* hot
господи́н; госпожа́ *gaspadin, gaspazha* Mr., Mrs., Miss; **господа́** *gaspada* gentlemen
гости́ница *gastinitsa* hotel
грибы́ *griby* mushrooms
гру́ша *groosha* pear

да *da* yes
дава́ть *davat* give; **да́йте!** *daitye!* give! **дава́йте** *davaitye* let's; **даю́т** *dayoot* they're doing (giving) (play, etc.)
дверь *dver* (f.) door
дворе́ц *dvaryets* palace
де́вушка *dyevooshka* girl, waitress

дежу́рная *dizhoornaya* corridor attendant
деклара́ция *diklaratsiya* declaration
де́лать *dyelat* do, make; **— сни́мки** — *snimki* take snapshots
де́ло *dyela* business, affair; **как дела́** *kak dyela*? How are things?; **по дела́м** *po dyelam* on business
день *dyen* (m.) day
де́ньги *dyengi* (pl.) money
дешёвый *dishoviy* (adj.) cheap; **деше́вле** *dishevle* cheaper
для *dlya* for
до *do* to, up to, as far as, before
до́брый/ая/ое/ые *dobriy/aya/aye/ye* good
до́лжен/должна́/должно́/должны́ *dolzhen/dulzhna/dulzhno/dulzhny* must
дом *dom* house; **до́ма** *doma* at home
дорого́й/а́я/о́е/и́е *darogoy/aya/oye/iye* expensive
до свида́ния *da svidaniya* good-bye
дре́вний/яя/ее/ие *drevniy/yaya/yeye/iye* ancient
друг *drook* friend (m.)
ду́мать *doomat* think; **я ду́маю** *ya doomayoo* I think

Евро́па *Yevropa* Europe
его́ *yevo* (acc. & gen.) him, it; his, its
еда́ *yeda* food
её *yeyo* (acc. & gen.) her, it; hers, its
ему́, ей *yemoo* ,*yei* (dat.) him, her
есть *yest* there is
е́хать *yekhat* to go (by transport)
ещё *yishcho* still, yet; **— оди́н** —*adin* another; **— раз** — *raz* again; **что — ?** *shto — ?* what else?

жаль *zhal* sorry
жа́рко *zharka* it's hot
жена́ *zhena* wife
же́нский *zhenskiy* (adj.) ladies'
жить *zhit* live; **я живу́** *ya zhivoo* I live
журна́л *zhoornal* magazine

за *za* at, (+ instr.) behind
заверни́те! *zavirnitye!* wrap it up!
за́втра *zaftra* tomorrow
заказа́ть *zakazat* order; **я заказа́л** *ya zakazal* I ordered
закрыва́ться *zakryvatsa* close (doors, museums)
закры́ть *zakryt* close
заку́ски *zakooski,* appetizers, snacks
заку́сочная *zakoosachnaya* snack bar
замеча́тельный/ая/ое/ые *zamichatyelniy/aya/aye/ye* wonderful, great
за́нят/занята́/за́нято/за́няты *zanyat/zanyata/zanyata/zanyaty* occupied, busy, taken
заплати́те! *zaplatitye!* pay!
запра́вочная коло́нка *zapravachnaya kalonka* service station
запреща́ется, запрещён *zaprishchaetsa, zaprishchon* (it's) forbidden
зате́м *zatyem* then
звони́ть *zvanit* phone
знать *znat* know
зову́т: меня́ — *zavoot: minya —* my name is

и *i* and
игра́ть *igrat* play
идти́ *ittee* go, be on (play); **я иду** *ya idoo* I go
из *iz* from, out of
извини́те *izvinitye* excuse me
икра́ *ikra* caviar
и́ли *ili* or
и́мя *imya* (first) name; **и́мени** *imeni* in the name of
интере́сный/ая/ое/ые *interyesniy/aya/aye/ye* interesting
их *ikh* them; their

к *k* to, toward
ка́жется *kazhitsa* it seems
как *kak* how
како́й/а́я/о́е/и́е *kakoi/aya/oye/iye* what, which
капу́ста *kapoosta* cabbage
ка́рта *karta* map
карто́фель *kartofil* (m.) potato

ка́рточка *kartachka* card, chit; **креди́тная —** *kreditnaya —* credit card
ка́сса *kassa* cashier
кафе́ *kafe* cafe
квита́нция *kvitantsiya* receipt
кино́ *kino* movie theater
кио́ск *kiosk* stand
ключ *klyooch* key
когда́ *kugda* when
ко́жа *kozha* leather
колбаса́ *kalbasa* sausage
конве́рт *kanvyert* envelope
коне́ц *kanyets* end
коне́чно *kanyeshna* of course
конфе́ты *kanfyety* candy
конце́рт *kantsert* concert
копе́йка/копе́йки/копе́ек *kapyeika/kapyeiki/kapeyek* kopeck(s)
кори́чневый *karichnyeviy* brown
коро́бка *karopka* box
кото́рый/ая/ое/ые *katoriy/aya/aye/ye* who, what, which; **— час?** *— chas?* what time is it?
ко́фе *kofi* coffee
краси́вый/ая/ое/ые *krasiviy/aya/aye/ye* beautiful, lovely
кра́сный/ая/ое/ые *krasniy/aya/aye/ye* red
Крым *Krym* Crimea
кто *kto* who; **— -то** *— -ta* someone
куда́ *kooda* where to
купальный костюм *koopalniy kastyoom* bathing suit
купа́ться *koopatsa* swim
купи́ть *koopeet* buy
кури́ть *kooreet* smoke
ку́рица *kooritsa* chicken

ле́вая (сторона́) *lyevaya (starana)* left (side)
ли *li* interrog. particle
лимо́н *limon* lemon; **с -ом** *s -am* with lemon
лимона́д *limanat* lemon-lime soft drink
ли́ния *liniya* line
литр *litr* liter
лифт *lift* elevator
ло́дка *lotka* boat
ло́жка *lozhka* spoon
лу́чше *loochshe* better, best
люби́ть *lyoobit* love; **я люблю** *ya looblyoo* I love
лю́ди *lyoodi* people

мавзоле́й *mavzolei* tomb, mausoleum
ма́ленький/ая/ое/ие *malinkiy/aya/aye/iye* little
ма́рка *marka* stamp; **5 ма́рок** *5 marak* 5 stamps
ма́сло *masla* butter
маши́на *mashina* car
ме́дленно *myedlinno* slowly
междунаро́дный *mizhdoonarodniy* international
меню́ *minyoo* menu
меня́/мне/мной *minya/mnye/mnoi* me
ме́сто *myesta* place, seat
метро́ *mitro* metro, subway
мёд *myod* honey; mead
милиционе́р *militsianer* policeman
минера́льная вода́ *mineralnaya vada* mineral water
мину́та *minoota* minute
мо́жет быть *mozhet byt* maybe
мо́жно *mozhna* one can, etc.
мой/моя́/моё/мои́ *moi/maya/mayo/mayee* (adj.) my
молодо́й/а́я/о́е/ы́е *maladoi/aya/oye/iye* young
молоко́ *malako* milk
моро́женое *marozhenaye* ice cream
Москва́ *Maskva* Moscow
мочь *moch* be able; **я могу** *ya magoo* I can
мужско́й *moozhskoi* (adj.) men's
музе́й *moozei* museum
му́зыка *moozyka* music
мы *my* we
мы́ло *myla* soap
мя́со *myasa* meat

на *na* for, to, on
на́до *nada* one ought, etc.
нале́во *nalyeva* to/on the left
напи́ток *napitak* drink; **напи́тки** *napitki* drinks
напиши́те! *napishitye!* Write (it) down
напра́во *naprava* to/on the right

напри́мер *naprimer* for example
напро́тив *naprotiv* opposite
нас/нам/на́ми *nas/nam/nami* us
нахо́дится *nakhoditsa* is situated
начи́наться *nachinatsa* begin (play, etc.)
наш/на́ша/наше/на́ши *nash/nasha/nashe/nashi* (adj.) our
недалеко́ *nidalyeko* not far
неде́ля *nidyelya* week
нельзя́ *nilzya* one can't, etc.
нет, не *nyet, ni* no, not
ничего́ *nichevo* nothing
но *no* but
но́вый/ая/ое/ые *noviy/aya/aye/ye* new
но́мер *nomir* (room) number
ночь *noch* (f.) night
нра́вится: мне — *nravitsa: mnye —* I like it
ну́жен/нужна́/ну́жно/нужны́ *noozhen/noozhna/noozhna/noozhny* have to, need; **мне ну́жно** *mnye noozhna* I need

о, об *o, ob,* about
обе́д *abyed* lunch
обме́н де́нег *abmyen dyenek* currency exchange
обменя́ть *abminyat* exchange
обра́тно *abratna* back
о́вощи *ovashchi* vegetables
огуре́ц *agooryets* cucumber
оде́жда *adyezhda* clothes
одея́ло *adiyalo* blanket
окно́ *akno* window
омле́т *amlyet* omelet
он, она́, оно́, они́ *on, ana, ano, ani* he (it), she (it), it, they
о́пера *opira* opera
орке́стр *arkestr* orchestra
осетри́на *asyetrina* sturgeon
оста́вить *astavit* leave, park (car)
остано́вка *astanofka* (bus, etc.) stop
от *ot* from
отвеча́ть *atvichat* answer
отде́л *atdyel* department
отдыха́ть *atdykhat* rest, go on vacation
открыва́ться *atkryvatsa* open (museums, etc.)
откры́тка *atkrytka* postcard
отли́чно *atlichna!* excellent!
отправле́ние *atpravleniye* departure
отправля́ться *atpravlyatsa* depart, set off
о́тпуск *otpoosk* vacation, leave; **в -е** *v -ye* on vacation
отходи́ть *atkhadit* leave, go away
о́чень *ochin* very
оши́бка *ashipka* mistake

па́мятник *pamyatnik* monument
папиро́са *papirosa* Russian cigarette
па́спорт *paspart* passport
пе́рвый/ая/ое/ые *pyerviy/aya/aye/ye* first
пе́ред *pyerid* before
переса́дка *pirisatka* connection, transfer **де́лать переса́дку** *dyelat pirisatkoo* change (train, etc.)
пи́во *piva* beer
пирожки́ *pirazhki* pies
пиро́жное *pirozhnaye* pastry; fancy cake
писа́ть *pisat* write
письмо́ *pismo* letter
пить *peet* drink
пла́вать *plavat* swim
пласти́нка *plastinka* record
плати́ть *platit* pay
плато́к *platok* head scarf
платфо́рма *platforma* platform
пла́тье *platye* dress
плёнка *plyonka* film
плохо́й/а́я/о́е/и́е *plokhoy/aya/oye/iye* bad **мне пло́хо** *mnye plokha* I feel ill
пло́щадь *ploshchad* (f.) square
пляж *plyazh* beach
по *po* along; **— -англи́йски** *— -angliiski* in English; **— -ру́сски** *— -russki* in Russian
повтори́те! *paftaritye!* repeat!
пого́да *pagoda* weather
пода́рки *padarki* gifts
подожди́те! *padazhditye!* wait!
подру́га *padrooga* friend (f.)
поду́шка *padooshka* pillow
подхо́дит: это вам — ? *padkhodit: eta vam — ?* Does that suit you?
по́езд *poyizd* train
пожа́луйста *pazhalasta* please, don't mention it

пойти́ (на бале́т) *paeetee (na balyet)* go (to the ballet)
пойдём(те) *paidyom(ti)* let's go
покажи́те! *pakazhitye!* show!
полови́на *palavina* half
полоте́нце *palatentse* towel
поме́рить *pamyerit* measure
помидо́ры *pamidory* tomatoes
понима́ть *panimat* understand; **я понима́ю** *ya panimayoo* I understand
пора́ *para* it's time
порекоменду́ете: что вы — ? *porikamendooitye: shto vy — ?* What do you recommend?; **я порекоменду́ю** *ya porikamendooyoo* I recommend
посеща́ть *pasyeshchat* visit
посла́ть *paslat* send
по́сле *posli* after
после́дний/яя/ее/ие *pasledniy/yaya/yeye/iye* last
посмотре́ть *pasmatryet* look at, see
посы́лка *pasylka* parcel
потеря́ть *patyeryat* lose
пото́м *patom* then
по́чта *pochta* post office
пра́вая (сторона́) *pravaya (starana)* right (side)
пра́вда *pravda* true, truth
прекра́сный/ая/ое/ые *prekrasniy/aya/aye,ye* fine, lovely
прибы́тие *pribytiye* arrival
приноси́ть: принесу́, принеси́те! *prinasit: prinisoo, prinisitye!* bring: I bring, bring!
приходи́ть: мы придём *prikhadit: my pridyom* come, arrive: we'll come
прия́тный/ая/ое/ые *priyatniy/aya/aye/ye* nice, pleasant
прода́жа *pradazha* sale; **про́даны** *prodany* (pl.) sold
прое́хать *prayekhat* get to (by transport)
пройти́ *praeetee* get to (on foot)
про́пуск *propoosk* (hotel) pass
проси́ть *prasit* ask, beg; **я прошу́ вас** *ya prashoo vas* I ask/beg you; **вас про́сят** *vas prosyat* you're wanted
прости́те *prastitye* forgive/excuse me
про́сто *prosta* simply, just — **пре́лесть** — *pryelist* simply delightful
прямо́й *pryamoi* (adj.) direct; **пря́мо** *pryama* straight on
путеводи́тель *pootivadityel* (m.) guidebook
пу́ть *poot* (m.) way, trip, path
пье́са *pyesa* play

рабо́тать *rabotat* work
рад/ра́да/ра́ды *rad/rada/rady* (m., f., pl.) glad, pleased (to meet you)
раз *raz* time; **три -а** *tree -a* three times
разгово́р *razgavor* conversation
разме́н, разменя́ть *razmyen, razminyat* change, exchange
разме́р *razmer* size
расписа́ние *raspisaniye* schedule
распиши́тесь! *raspishityes!* sign!
рестора́н *ristaran* restaurant
рис *rees* rice
родили́сь: вы — *radilis: vy* — you were born
ро́зовый/ая/ое/ые *rozaviy/aya/aye/ye* pink, rosé
Росси́я *Rassiya* Russia
рот *rot* mouth
руба́шка *roobashka* shirt
рубль/рубли́/рубля́/рубле́й *roobl/roobli/rooblya/rooblyei* ruble
ру́сский/ая/ое/ие *roosskiy/aya/aye/iye* (adj.) Russian
ры́ба *ryba* fish
ряд *ryad* row
ря́дом *ryadam* next to, near

с, со *s, so* with, from
сади́тесь! *sadityes!* sit down!
сала́т *salat* salad
самова́р *samavar* samovar
самолёт *samalyot* airplane
сапоги́ *sapagi* boots
са́хар *sakhar* sugar
светофо́р *svyetafor* traffic lights
сви́тер *sviter* sweater
свобо́дно *svabodno* (it's) free, vacant
сда́ча *sdacha* change

сего́дня *sivodnya* today; **-шний** *-shniy* (adj.) today's
сейча́с *syichas* at once, right away
сельдь *syeld* (f.) herring
се́рдце *sertse* heart
середи́на *siridina* middle
сига́ра *sigara* cigar
сигаре́та *sigareta* cigarette
сиде́ть *seedyet* sit, suit (clothes)
симпати́чный/ая/ое/ые *seempatichniy/aya/aye/ye* nice, pleasant (person)
си́ний/яя/ее/ие *siniy/yaya/yeye/iye* blue
скажи́те! *skazhitye!* say! **вы ска́жете мне?** *vy skazhitye mnye?* Will you tell me?
ско́лько *skolka* how much/many
сла́дкое *sladkaye* dessert
сле́дующий/ая/ее/ие *sledooyooshchiy/aya/eye/iye* next, following
сли́шком *slishkam* too
слу́шать *slooshat* listen; **слу́шаю** *slooshayoo* I'm listening
смета́на *smitana* sour cream
смотри́те! *smatritye!* look!
собо́р *sabor* cathedral
сове́тский/ая/ое/ие *savyetskiy/aya/aye/iye* (adj.) Soviet
совсе́м *savsyem* quite; **— не** — *ni* not at all
согла́сны *saglasny* (pl.) agreed
сожале́нию: к *sazhalyeniyoo: k* unfortunately
сок *sok* juice
со́лнце *solntsi* sun; **со́лнечно** *solnichniy* (adj.) sunny
соси́ска *sasiska* sausage
спаси́бо *spaseeba* thank you
сперва́ *spirva* at first
споко́йный/ая/ое/ые *spakoiniy/aya/aye/ye* calm, peaceful
спорти́вный/ая/ое/ые *spartivniy/aya/aye,ye* (adj.) sports
спра́вочное бюро *spravachnaya byooro* information office
сра́зу *srazoo* at once
стака́н *stakan* glass
ста́нция *stantsiya* station
ста́рый/ая/ое/ые *stariy/aya/aye/ye* old
сто́ит/сто́ят *stoit/stoyat* costs, cost
стол *stol* table
столи́ца *stalitsa* capital
столо́вая *stalovaya* dining room, snack bar
сторона́ *starana* side
стоя́нка такси́ *stayanka taksi* taxi stand
сты́дно *stydna* ashamed
су́мка *soomka* bag; **су́мочка** *soomachka* handbag
сухо́й *sookhoi/aya/oye/iye* dry
схе́ма *skhema* diagram, map
сходи́ть *skhadit* get out (of vehicle)
счёт *shchyot* account, bill, abacus
сыр *syr* cheese
сюда́ *syooda* here (hither)

таба́к *tabak* tobacco shop
та́кже *takzhe* also
такси́ *taksi* taxi
тало́н(ы) *talon(y)* voucher(s)
там *tam* there
теа́тр *tiatr* theater
телефо́н *tilifon* telephone
тепе́рь *tipyer* now
това́рищ *tavarishch* comrade
тогда́ *tugda* then
то́же *tozhe* also, too
то́лько *tolka* only
тот/та/то/те *tot/ta/to/tye* (adj.) this, these
то́чно *tochna* precisely
трамва́й *tramvai* streetcar
тролле́йбус *trallyeibus* trolley
туале́т *twalyet* toilet
туда́ *tooda* there (thither)
ты/тебя́/тебе́/тобо́й *ty/tibya/tibye/taboi* you (fam.)

у *oo* in the possession of, at the home of **— меня́** — *minya* I have
уви́дите *oovidityе* you will see
уго́дно: что вам — ? *oogodna: shto vam — ?* What would you like?
у́гол: на углу́ *oogal: na oogloo* at the corner
удиви́тельно *oodivityelna* it's wonderful

удово́льствие: с -м *oodavolstviye: s -m* with pleasure
ужа́сно *oozhasna* it's dreadful
у́жин *oozhin* supper
у́лица *oolitsa* street
у́тро *ootra* morning; **-м** *-m* in the morning
учи́тель *oochityel* teacher

фами́лия *familiya* surname
фильм *film* film
фотоаппара́т *fotaapparat* camera
фотографи́ровать *fatagrafiravat* to photograph
фру́кты *frookty* (pl.) fruit; **фрукто́вый** *frooktovy* (adj.) fruit
фунт, фу́нты *foont, foonty* pound, pounds
футбо́л *footbol* soccer

хлеб *khlyep* bread
хокке́й *khakkei* (ice) hockey
холо́дный/ая/ое/ые *khalodniy/aya/aye/ye* cold
хоро́ший/ая/ее/ые *kharoshiy/aya/eye/iye* good
хорошо́ *kharasho* fine, OK
хоте́ть *khotet* want; **я хочу** *ya khachoo* I want; **хотите?** *khatitye?* Do you want?
хо́чется: мне — *khochitsa: mnye* — I feel like

цвет *tsvyet* color; **с цвета́ми** *s tsvyetami* with flowers
цена́ *tsena* price
центр *tsentr* center; **— го́рода** —*gorada* town center
центра́льный *tsentralniy* (adj.) central

це́рковь *tserkof* (f.) church
цирк *tsirk* circus

чай *chai* tea
час *chas* hour, o'clock; **-ы** *-y* (pl.) watch
ча́шка *chashka* cup
чек *chek* receipt
челове́к *chelavyek* person
чемода́н *chemadan* suitcase
чемпиона́т *chempionat* championship
че́рез *cheryez* after
чёрный/ая/ое/ые *chorniy/aya/aye/ye* black
что *shto* what, that; **— ещё** — *yishcho* anything else; — **-нибу́дь (то)** — *-niboot (to)* something (for)
чу́вствовать: чу́вствую себя́ *choostvavat: choostvuyoo sibya* I feel
чуде́сно *choodyesna* it's wonderful

шипу́чий/ая/ее/ие *shipoochiy/aya/yeye/iye* sparkling
шокола́д *shakalat* chocolate; **шокола́дный** *shakaladniy* (adj.) chocolate

экску́рсия *ekskoorsiya* excursion
эта́ж *etazh* floor, storey
э́то *eta* it's
э́тот/э́та/э́то/э́ти *etat/eta/eta/eti* (adj.) this, these

я *ya* I
я́блоко *yablaka* apple
яи́чница *yaichnitsa* fried eggs
яйцо́, я́йца *yaitso, yaitsa* egg, eggs
язы́к *yazyk* language